SONGS FROM AN IMPERFECT LIFE

SONGS FROM AN IMPERFECT LIFE

J. Ronald M. York
author of Kept in the Dark

Best Wishes!
Ron York

Songs From an Imperfect Life
J. Ronald M. York
p. cm.

ISBN 978-0-9982734-4-0

This book is printed on acid-free paper.

First Edition

visit www.JRonaldMYork.com

ACKNOWLEDGEMENTS

This book would not have been possible without the
help and guidance from
Mary Helen Clarke, Ralph Henley, Trish Luna,
Jade Reynolds,
Julie Schoerke and Lynette Sesler

Or the continued love and support from
Tom Collins, Erin Daunic, Bing Davis, Donna Pence, Carol Poston,
Jeremy Rochford, Al Sherick and Miriam Tate

Cover concept and author photo by
Jade Reynolds

For those who have spent their lives holding secrets…

One thought keeps flashing through my mind:
What memories of our life do we leave behind?

INTRODUCTION

BOX OF LETTERS

It was just an innocuous liquor box that had been stored in a trunk and placed under the work bench, in the detached shed behind my childhood home. And yet, its contents caused my life to take a detour.

The box held 200 letters, exchanged between my parents in 1955-56, along with newspaper clippings, photos and cards from friends. This time capsule revealed a crime to which my father had pleaded guilty, and it set the wheels in motion for our family to leave our home in Miami and start over in Tennessee. I was 2, turning 3 years old, and have absolutely no recollection of the events described in my parents' letters. This was never discussed in our household, and I am not aware of any of my relatives, or our Florida friends, ever mentioning the box in front of me.

So, at age 47, with my parents and many relatives gone, I found out my dad had been accused of molesting boys in the Scout troop in which he had served as Scoutmaster, at Central Baptist church in Miami.

Opening that box, I saw envelopes addressed to my mother at our former Miami address, along with envelopes addressed to my dad, care of Dade County Jail. I also spotted a yellowed newspaper clipping, from the *Miami Herald*, with the headline: *Boy Fondler*.

I was in the process of going through the contents of our family home to prepare for an estate sale after my father's sudden death from injuries sustained in a single car accident in July 2000. My mother had passed away in 1985 from the ravages of cancer. Friends were helping me on that day, so I said nothing, and quickly closed the box. I placed it in my car before anyone noticed or questioned my discovery.

I have been asked if I ever thought my parents intended for me to see what that box held, and my answer is yes. That box moved with us from Miami to Chattanooga in 1956, and then on to Nashville in 1957. In fact, it moved with us to three different houses in Nashville. I have also been asked if I thought my mother kept it without my dad's knowledge. My answer is no.

I truly believe it was saved for me to find. The crime had been covered in the newspaper as well as TV — as referenced in one of the letters. Family and friends were well aware of it, so there was always the possibility of me finding out. By saving their letters, exchanged while they were apart, they left behind, in their own words, their thoughts and how they struggled to survive and eventually make amends. The box's contents offer a clearer and more rounded insight into their ordeal.

At the time of my discovery, I was overwhelmed in dealing with the family estate issues caused by my father's sudden death. There was no time to focus on what I had found, so the box remained stored in my garage. Whenever I would notice the box sitting on the shelf, I would rationalize that I needed to wait until I could find the time to devote to reading each letter, and piecing the story together.

Then at age 63, I saw the award-winning movie, *Spotlight*. The movie, dealing with the Catholic priest sex abuse scandal, left me an emotional wreck by the time the closing credits rolled. I had seen movies, plays and television shows that dealt with the subject of sexual abuse, and was often moved to tears, but after this movie I found myself hysterically crying, in my home alone. Maybe it was the fact that this was based on a true story, or maybe I had finally reached the point in my life where childhood memories began to flood my mind. Regardless, it became the catalyst that made me want to know my dad's story and how it might relate to my own. I emptied the contents of the box on my dining room table, and used the envelopes' postmarks to begin the process of reading their letters chronologically.

I learned that my father was not the only one accused. His assistant Scoutmaster, who was a close friend, had also been accused. I found that most of the charges brought were against his friend. My father had just one charge, which unfortunately came from my uncle on behalf of my 13-year-old cousin, the oldest son of my mother's older sister.

I kept everything to myself for the next two months, which left me in a very dark place emotionally. When my closest friend had finally had enough of my behavior, she bluntly asked: "What the hell is wrong with you?"

Once I started talking, I could not stop. I had to get it all out of my system, and by doing so, I realized that I could finally pull myself out of the story. Up until that point, I would lose myself in my parents' words, which described how they tried to deal with the circumstances in which they found themselves. My dear mother struggled to make life normal for me, her 2-year-old son. I also thought that the letters told an amazing story. They revealed the love and devotion between my parents, Bob and Joyce York.

I made the choice to share what I had found. And yet, since this crime had never been a part of my life, I realized that I would also need to offer the version of the Bob and Joyce that I knew. As an artist, composer, designer and gallery owner, I had never seen myself as a writer, but now I had a story to tell.

Kept in the Dark is the result of my desire — and yes, my need — to tell of my parents' love, as well as their journey. However, I could not reveal that my father was accused of sexually abusing a minor, without revealing that, as a minor, I was also sexually abused.

Hating the word "victim," I choose to say that I am a survivor. But now I wonder, at what cost? I never told my parents of the abuse. It was my secret, and I always felt that I had it handled. I had equated having kept silent, with having "come to terms with," but I was mistaken. Because my parents shared their story with me after their deaths through the contents of that liquor box, I finally found the strength to share my own story.

During my junior high and high school years, I wrote poetry — and by my senior year in high school, I had put a few of those poems to music. My songwriting continued through several decades, and often I'd record these snippets of my life. Then I stepped away from music for several years, but returned when I turned 60.

I was never one to journal my feelings or keep a diary, but now I realize, through my poems and song lyrics, that I unknowingly had been keeping a journal all along. Scraps of paper, backs of envelopes, and pages torn from a three-ring binder — my collected thoughts through the years. A box of old cassette tapes reveal the anguish in my voice as I sang, played the piano, and escaped my life for just a few minutes.

Now I share with you bits and pieces of an imperfect and complicated life, often hidden by a smiling facade, as I interject a line, verse, refrain, or even the lyrics to an entire song. Those words will help fill in the emotions that I have often tried to keep inside.

I catch a glimpse, now and then.
You know the mind plays tricks,
You just can't win.
You think you're safe, no more pain,
Then you close your eyes,
And it starts again.

FOREWORD

"That which has been believed by everyone, always and everywhere, has every chance of being false." — Paul Valery

Exposing one's innermost thoughts is difficult. Disclosing the personal events that have occurred in one's life — the good, the bad and the ugly — is beyond the ability of most people. Yet Ron York has made a heartfelt, soul-wrenching attempt to do so. Starting with multiple episodes as a young victim of child sexual abuse by a variety of perpetrators, to his high-risk sexual behaviors as an adolescent and adult, the link between early sexualization and its short- and long-term effects is a recurrent theme made real in these pages.

As someone who grew up with Ron, went to church with him and dated him in adolescence, I thought I knew him well. He always had a smile on his face, seemed happy and well adjusted. He had "perfect" parents, lived in a well-to-do neighborhood, and had plenty of friends. He was funny, a bit adventuresome, and a guy I always felt I could talk to. We grew apart in late adolescence, only meeting occasionally at church or when I sought his help in decorating my first house. In 2016, we reconnected and started to catch up. Talking with him prior to the publication of his first book, *Kept in the Dark*, I realized how very little I knew of his life and family and the doubts and demons that traveled daily with him. He, on the other hand, knew little of my world as a Special Agent with the Tennessee Bureau of Investigation, with an expertise in sexual abuse — specifically, child sexual abuse.

As I read this manuscript I was surprised, but not shocked, by the personal disclosures of the depth and chronicity of Ron's choices and sexual behaviors. It is fairly common for individuals who have been sexualized as children to engage in high-risk sexual behaviors as adolescents and adults. His lack of reasonable consideration as to the possible consequences of such activities is also common. The fact that these events occurred in the 1960s, '70s, and '80s — as the world of gays and lesbians were radically changing, with little in the way of guidelines to assist them — allowed for a wide range of sexual acting out, with little inhibition. Few questioned what was "normal" versus "troubling" sexual behaviors.

What overcame my professional detachment from his description of a chaotic personal life is the realization of the pain Ron has carried for the vast majority of his life, from an innocent 7-year-old boy to the man he is today. Pain he did not, could not share with anyone, pain and longing for stable and loving relationships. He daily wore a mask of normalcy and cheerfulness. He succeeded in several careers. He is a wonderfully creative musician and artist. Yet the burden of maintaining a false front for so long has come at a heavy cost. As the secrets of his father and mother were revealed in *Kept in the Dark*, the need to peel away the layers of his own hidden life became overwhelming. Ron is a complex, complicated, very talented, loving man with amazing resiliency. I love him for who he was, is, and will become as his journey continues.

Please read this book with the compassion Ron, and others who have had similar paths, deserve. For those who say, "I would never do that!" — remember that all of us live in glass houses. We just keep the blinds closed so the light of our actions is never exposed to others, and perhaps, not even to ourselves.

— Donna M. Pence, Special Agent,
Tennessee Bureau of Investigation, retired

PROLOGUE

With a bag of popcorn in my hand, I made my way down the dimly-lit aisle to find my seat in the middle of an empty row near the front of the cavernous movie theater. It wasn't long before someone older sat in the row behind me and began talking to me before the coming attractions started to roll. Once he was sure I was alone, he asked if he could join me.

At age 10, I was already familiar with the routine that would begin with his leg touching mine, his hand grazing my knee before working its way up my thigh. This was not my first time, nor would it be my last.

SONGS FROM
AN IMPERFECT LIFE

ONE

JESUS LOVES ME

AGE 7

I have a church bulletin from Miami's Central Baptist Church, dated September 19, 1952, with my mother's photo on the front. It announces her resignation, after seven years, as the church's Educational Secretary. The reason given for her departure: to assume the position of "full-time Christian mother." I was born three months later. My dad's arrest for sexually abusing boys within the church-sponsored Scout troop followed two years after my birth. During that difficult time, both emotionally and financially, my mother took a part-time secretary job at a sister Baptist church in Miami until our home was sold and we were able to move to Tennessee.

Our family became members of Nashville's First Baptist Church in 1956. As was our church in Miami, First Baptist is located downtown, with a congregation that comes from all areas of the city. The church

*First Baptist Church
Nashville, Tennessee*

was two blocks from the Christian Life Commission, where my mother worked, and the downtown shopping district, where I spent childhood summers. The church had, and still does have, a large campus made up of several connected buildings. When we joined, it was anchored by the 1886 sanctuary building that was replaced by the time I graduated high school. They did save the Gothic steeple tower, as a tie to the past. My parents would often arrive early because of certain responsibilities such as committee meetings, which would allow me to join other kids freely roaming the hallways.

I aimlessly wandered through those buildings, from basement to top floor, as a child. I can't imagine there was much of anything that I did not explore, either alone or with friends. I remember clearly the wood floors and steps that would creak in the older of the two educational buildings. I spent many years climbing those steps to my classrooms, or descending to the basement level for the weekly Wednesday night supper. Those meals would consist of a meat, often referred to by my dad as "mystery meat," and assorted vegetables and a dessert. Rows of adjoining rectangular folding tables filled the room. I was expected to sit with my parents until I was older and could join my classmates.

The newer of the church buildings had floors of waxed linoleum tiles and were positioned on the opposite end of the block from the ancient sanctuary. The nursery, library, and church offices were on the first floor, while the other levels consisted of classrooms surrounding larger open meeting rooms. Most of these areas were occupied on Sundays. However, many remained empty and dark during the less-crowded Wednesday night activities, which then provided the perfect time to explore.

The spookiest part of the church to me as a child was the sanctuary building. It had dark wood floors with deep red carpet, and pews with scratchy red velvet cushions. Although there was no assigned seating in our church, each family had chosen its own place to gather for services. Our family always sat on the organ side to the right, facing the pulpit.

There was something dark and eerie to me about the room that held the choir robes, and the narrow hall and steps leading to the Baptismal pool. I also remember, all too well, the men's restroom just outside of that area — old, small, and private for later sexual encounters. As creepy as some of those places felt to a child, it never deterred any of us from checking them out.

One Seventh Avenue entrance had a staircase leading to the balcony. The stairs continued up another level to an always-locked door. The street entrance on the opposite side of the sanctuary had a door that was occasionally locked, and revealed a tiny wooden spiral stairway leading up to the steeple and attic area, above the balcony. I would venture to say there were very few kids who did not make that climb at some point.

Another mysterious area was a door off the balcony, on the piano side of the pulpit. I would often try the door, only to find it locked. My curiosity would turn to frustration. Eventually, I did find the door unlocked, and the two isolated classroom spaces were revealed. It was a letdown, but it turned out to be a great hiding spot when I wanted to disappear!

To a young child, it was exciting to have so many areas to explore. I never thought about the fact that anyone could have come in off the street and be afforded a safe and secure hiding place. Of course, it did not appear that this alarmed anyone.

The fact is, perhaps we actually should have been more fearful of some of the church members among us.

I was 7-years-old when I was first molested at church. This was three years after we moved from Miami, because my dad had been accused of the same crime. I remember the man who did it, because he continued as a member of our church for many years after our encounter. He was probably in his mid-20s at that time and, I believe, unmarried.

Seven-year-old Ron with his dad, Bob

It happened in the Children's Primary Department, where I attended Sunday School on Sunday mornings, and Training Union on Sunday nights. The area was on the second floor in the older central building of the church. I don't remember anyone else being around, which, no doubt, allowed him to be comfortable with what he was doing.

Although the encounters continued, I never felt afraid. He was nice, showed me attention, and never hurt me. He would undo my trousers, pull them down, and then proceed to touch me. Whether he was nervous, or just wanted to keep me calm, I remember that he would keep talking to me. Eventually, he would pull my pants back up, often give me a dime and, sometimes, a hug. I don't remember feeling in danger, which may be why I did not run, or tell anyone.

This routine happened several more times. Eventually, he would unzip his pants in the process. He never asked me to do anything to him and seemed perfectly content just to caress me. I have tried to remember why it stopped, and I cannot come up with a reason, other than maybe he found someone new.

The Children's Primary Department was an area of the church that I was not only familiar with, but also made me feel comfortable and safe.

As an adult, I can now look back at the 7-year-old me and reflect on the secret I kept from everyone. While I do not remember being warned to keep silent, I imagine that is what happened. Discipline was strict in our home. Punishment from my dad could come by way of a belt or a switch off of a tree. I have to think that if I had been instructed not to tell my parents, I would have obeyed for fear that I would be in trouble for my actions.

I now realize that my parents and I lived parallel lies as we perfected the art of keeping secrets. We were actors playing our roles as the perfect suburban family — living day to day, somewhere between the lies. But in truth, the child was sexually abused. The father escaped incarceration for the same crime, to which he pled guilty, leaving the mother to play her truest role by holding her family together with her steadfast love and her iron will. Unlike me, my parents never had the chance to remove their masks during their lifetimes. They must have felt they always had to keep up appearances, lest someone suspect something amiss in their ideal world.

For me, my life changed at age 7 — my innocence stolen.

I've blocked the memory out of my day,
And I told myself, it's better this way.

But still somehow, when I fall asleep,
Into my dreams, painful memories still creep.

♫

I am also blessed with good memories of my time in the Children's Primary Department at our church — memories that became even more special as I became an adult.

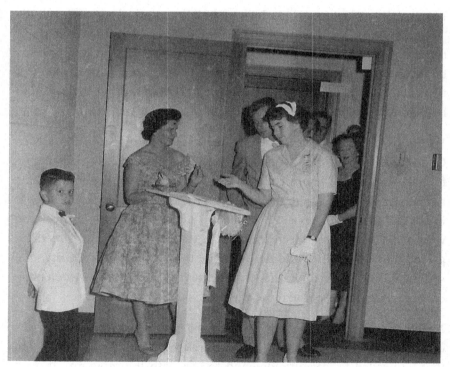

Seven-year-old Ron with his mother, Joyce

One of my favorite people from my days at First Baptist Church was Miss Helen Conger. She was what some people might describe as an old maid. Because of a cleft lip, she had a distinctive nasal speaking voice, plus a feisty personality that I came to appreciate much later in life. Her "day job" was the first full-time librarian at the Baptist Sunday School Board. However, I knew her as director of our church's Primary Children's Department.

In working with children, Miss Conger would figure out what they enjoyed, try to cultivate it, then engage the children and spark their interests. If a child liked music, she would ask that child to help select the hymns to sing. If they enjoyed reading, she would encourage them to read our weekly Bible verses out loud, and so on.

For me, she picked up on my love of design and asked me to create the "interest center" each week. Now, an interest center consisted of going through a box of assorted fabric scraps and finding one to drape across the front table, along with choosing a flower arrangement or candlestick to display with an open Bible. For this young boy, who in later years would have a successful interior design career, it was a pretty big deal.

When I was in my 30s and with my mother struggling with cancer, Miss Conger would visit me at our family's Christmas store, often bringing food. As an adult, I had the chance to get to know her better and came to love her even more. She shared with me a story from back when I was in her children's department. It seems my dad had had a stern discussion with her regarding me "decorating" each week. He felt it was something geared more to girls. He did not want me to be a "sissy." (Of course, that ship had already sailed.) Rather than simply asking her if she would stop encouraging me, he told her that was what she was going to do.

Needless to say, Miss Conger — God love her — was not one to back down. She told my dad that I enjoyed creating the interest centers, and that he needed to leave it alone and to "get with the program." It must have worked, because my dad never said anything to me about it, and I continued working my magic. ... or as much magic as an 8-year-old can do with a box of fabric scraps and artificial flowers.

When my mother died in 1985, Miss Conger sent me the most beautiful heartfelt letter. Two years later, when she passed away, my dad made arrangements for her cemetery plot to be beside our family's plot.

♫

What caused me to crave attention? How did I become an easy target for the men in our church? Was it because I desperately wanted to be noticed, so I allowed the fondling to happen when I could have easily run away or told someone? Am I at fault? Common and legal sense would say no. I was a minor, and regardless of my actions or responses, an adult should not have allowed anything to happen. But it feels to me as if I were a willing participant … or later became one.

This is why I think of my life as a series of contradictions: Religion and the Southern Baptist church was at the heart of my upbringing. Yet early in that upbringing, when I was just a child, I was introduced to sex within the walls of my Southern Baptist church.

On the church's current website, I found this quote: "At First Kids, we believe children are one of God's greatest blessings to all of us. We have awesome programs for kids of all ages that will teach them about Jesus in a fun and safe environment."

I know that many safeguards are now in place to prevent what happened to me and others from happening again. After all, that was more than 50 years ago. Still, I can't help but wonder what my life would have been like had I been warned to stay away from those men at church. How would my life have been different if I had not had sexual encounters as a child?

T W O

MOVIE LOVER

AGE 10

Downtown Nashville in the 1950s and 1960s was much different from the landscape of today. I remember residential areas being limited to only a few apartment buildings. Some people chose to live in the aging hotels such as the Sam Davis, the Savoy and the Hermitage. Two high-rise apartment buildings, Capitol Towers and Metro Manor, came on the scene in the early 1960s. What our downtown did have was a thriving shopping district. Now, more than 50 years later, apartments and condos are everywhere, but the downtown is severely lacking in the shopping conveniences it once had.

We moved to Nashville in 1956. My dad's office was in the Exchange Building on Church Street between Third and Fourth Avenues. My mother's office was in the Frost Building on Eighth, one block from Church Street. By 1963, my dad's office had moved to the midtown area of Broadway,

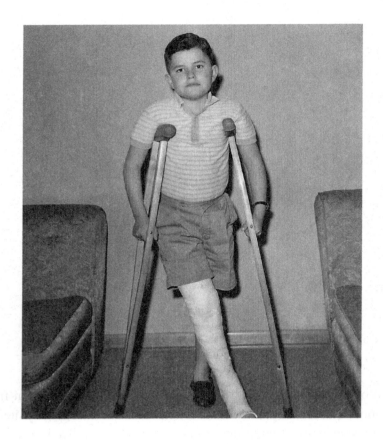

and my mother's office into the Southern Baptist Convention's stylish new octagon-shaped building on James Robertson Parkway.

My childhood summers were often spent going to work with my mom. By midmorning, I'd be allowed to walk a few short blocks over to Church Street and spend my days going to movies and rummaging through department stores. You could find three large locally-owned departments stores in a four-block stretch, including Cain-Sloan, Harvey's and Castner Knott. There was also a W.T. Grant store, with the upper floors housing Watkins College of Art — where, years later, I served on their Board of Trustees. Furniture stores such as Payne's and Percy Cohen could be found on Third Avenue, as well as others such as Sterchi's, Beesley's and Harley-Holt a couple of blocks south on Broadway.

Grand movie houses lined the main street of our downtown shopping district. During my childhood summers, my parents felt I was not old enough to stay home alone while they worked. Both parents' jobs were downtown, so I would often go to work with them. When the stores and theaters came to life about 10 in the morning, I would be given money and head out alone to explore. Often I would escape into those dark, voluminous theaters and settle in for a double feature. I was never by myself for long.

The Tennessee Theater was a wonderful Art Deco building, and it was the largest theater with more than 2,000 seats. It was elegant, and although it had been lovingly restored, it met its demise in the late 1980s. The most unique theater was the Loews Vendome. Originally an opera house with 1,600 seats, it boasted two balconies and 16 orchestra boxes. Unfortunately, it burned in 1967 and Loews took over the less architecturally interesting Crescent Theater. With only 850 seats, it was one of the smallest theaters, although it offered the widescreen Cinerama technology that was all the rage then.

The Knickerbocker Theater was a few doors off of Church Street and had entrances on both Sixth Avenue and Capitol Boulevard. I was 9 years old when it closed in 1961, and yet I can remember seeing a couple of movies there alone.

Walt Disney said, "Movies can and do have tremendous influence in shaping young lives in the realm of entertainment towards the ideals and objectives of normal adulthood."

My mother wrote my father a letter on November 30, 1955, while he was in jail awaiting trial after being accused of molesting my 13-year-old cousin.

She told him that she took me to a movie, and that after the newsreel, cartoon and short, my eyes were starting to close, so we left. The movie was Walt Disney's *The African Lion*. I was 2-years-old and have no memory of that day, but I imagine that I am one of many whose inaugural movie experience was something from Disney Studios.

The first movie I actually remember seeing has stayed with me for more than 50 years. I was 10 years old at the time and visiting my grandmother in Miami. I remember the title of the movie as *Hippodrome*, and the story revolved around circus performers. I also remember the leading actor and that his character's name was Rudy. Although puberty doesn't usually begin until about age 11, I felt an unexplained attraction to him and convinced my grandmother to sit through the movie for a second time. *Hippodrome* had an impact on me that I still feel today. I have tried, without luck, to find a copy of the movie. I'll admit that there is a part of me that fears that the illusion I have held on to for all of these years will be lost by seeing the movie now, as an adult.

In searching for the film, I did find movie stills and posters. Finding these helped make sense of the emotion I felt. I've also found reviews, such as this one from The New York Times in 1962: "The movie's real asset is its picturesque coziness in trailing a small troupe of specialty performers around various arenas, supper clubs and hippodromes. Three of them: a handsome tiger trainer, a beautiful dancer, and a sharp-shooter with a Svengalian air, tangle romantically and professionally."

Hippodrome is an "Austrian-made backstage drama" released in 1959. An English-dubbed version made its way to the States in 1962. The movie poster boasts, "Trixie wanted success at any cost!" and, "Rudy was more faithful to his beasts than to her!" I realize now, after recently seeing a movie still, that what I was feeling had much to do with the "handsome tiger trainer" and his wardrobe that consisted of not much more than a leopard-skin Speedo.

A second movie from 1962 has stayed with me and, once again, I had gone with my grandmother. I'm sure she saw the names of the screen legends in the billing and did not think much about the actual story. The movie was *Whatever Happened to Baby Jane?* Even at age 10, I think I recognized it for the gem that it was. High drama — high camp. No Disney princesses for me — my childhood memories involve aging, bickering screen goddesses.

Walt Disney may have said that movies help influence young lives toward the ideals of "normal adulthood," but inside those theaters, as the movies played, my childhood became far from normal.

It was the summer of 1964, and I had just finished sixth grade. But now I was a child sitting alone in an empty theater. I can understand how that had to have been very tempting to men prone to pedophilia, and since I appeared receptive, men with eager hands would take a seat next to me.

I loved to disappear into a dark theater, and remember that the middle of a summer day would net less than a dozen patrons sprinkled throughout the vast first floor — balconies would be closed off until the evening hours.

I did not go to meet anyone, but it was rare when someone did not approach me. Some men were more forward than others, but most were kind as they tried to make me feel special. A few would ask me to follow them into the restroom, where they were more comfortable as they unzipped my pants.

As I said, this was not new or even frightening to me. I had learned what to expect from earlier encounters that had taken place within my church over the years, with three different men. I think I can now admit to myself that the more it happened, the more I wanted the attention.

I realize that saying, "I wanted the attention" could leave the impression that my parents were distant or absent from my life. That was not the case at all. They were loving, generous and often doting. I always had a strong bond with my mother and loved being around her. I think what I'm trying to convey is that the added attention afforded me a feeling that may have been like a drug. The more I received, the more I craved.

I now know the terminology is called "grooming." The seducer latches onto someone (a child in this scenario), whom he makes feel special, wanted, needed and — yes — desired. It's a feeling that most of us enjoy: the center of attention. When it progresses to a sexual situation, children are often passive, not wanting the special feeling to end. It may appear that they are willing, when the truth may be that they really just don't understand. Being exposed to sex at such a young age is confusing. Plus, I was too young for the men's actions to be sexually satisfying for me.

I did not know the names of the men then. But as I grew older, I would see a few pictured in the newspaper or at a charity fundraiser and learned that they were married men with respectable jobs and families. In fact, just recently, I served on a committee with the daughter of one of my abusers.

Her father is now deceased, and I knew that nothing would be gained by telling her about her dad's involvement in my fractured childhood.

The most memorable theater for me back then was the Paramount. I thought it was unique, because you entered on the balcony level and walked down a wide staircase to the main floor. With 2,000 seats, it was the second-largest downtown theater. One of the things I distinctly remember was the ironwork over the exit doors on each side of the screen. There were nude, oversized, female statues perched on ledges above the exits in front of a decorative grill.

In 1965, the Paramount hosted a screening of the Billy Graham film, *The Restless Ones*. I remember several things about that event, the most comical thing being that they draped the nude statues for fear someone would be offended. But as I sat there, at age 13, along with my parents and all of the "Fine Christian folk" watching a Billy Graham film, I could not help but think about the dozens of times I was molested in that very same theater during the previous three summers.

THREE

YOUNG & RESTLESS

AGES 12-14

I did not spend all of my summer months in dark theaters. I would also walk up and down Church Street, wander through department stores, and grab a hot dog or hamburger at one of the various luncheon counters. In fact, it was at the luncheonette on the lower level of the W.T. Grant store that I saw a familiar face from a past movie experience. He noticed me, too, and took the stool next to mine at the counter. I don't remember much of the conversation, but when we had finished eating, he asked if I needed to use the restroom. I did, but I was not blind to where this would lead.

In the 1960s, you would often see pay toilets in public restrooms. I remember some restrooms in which all of the stalls had a coin lock on the doors, and others that might have a few free stalls, and only one or two that were locked. My understanding was that this helped to offset maintenance costs. The W.T. Grant store had two men's restrooms, side by side. Each of

them had a pay lock, which was on the outside door and cost a dime to enter. The restrooms had a sink, urinal and toilet stall. After putting a dime in the lock, my "friend" opened the door to an empty and private space.

My body had begun to respond to sex, which excited my seducer. I did not reciprocate, but I did let him enjoy himself. When he was done, and we both were pulling up our pants, a noise startled me, and I realized that someone else had put a coin into the door and was in the process of coming in. As soon as he heard that, he pushed me back into the stall and closed the door. Not being able to see, I did not realize that he had then left as the other man entered. With my pants and belt fastened, I flushed the toilet and stepped out to wash my hands. The new visitor was at the urinal and looked at me with interest. I left quickly, but continued to think about what had just happened and what could clearly happen again.

With my newfound knowledge and raging hormones, I concluded that I could have sex any time I wanted, whether it was at church, a movie theater or public restroom. This was my secret, along with the realization that I had the power. Men wanted me, coveted me, and I liked that feeling. There were, though, some men who showed no interest in me at all, and I couldn't understand why. I realize now that they were smart enough to stay clear of someone underage. But, at the time, it left me wondering what was wrong with me. The attention I had felt at age 7, from the first man who had touched me at church, was now available to me whenever I chose. It became an addiction. And as a 12-year-old, I was not aware what a harmful path I was on.

I discovered other outlets downtown that were available for an easy encounter. One day I ate at the luncheonette on the lower level of Harvey's department store. The men's room was in clear sight from where I sat, and I watched men come and go. After I finished eating, I went into the restroom and found all of the stalls occupied, along with a couple of men, side by side, at the urinals. When a stall opened up, I went in and sat down. I could see through the crack where the door was hinged, the men at the urinal checking each other out. Being so engrossed in what I saw, I was caught off guard when a hand reached under the partition and motioned to me. At first I was frightened, but then realized he was making a move

on me. I leaned down and peered under the partition to see a man fully aroused. Not knowing how things were usually done, I decided to exit with the knowledge that this was another possible spot for the attention I had begun to crave.

Before the summer of 1964 was over and I entered seventh grade, I had learned that there were many places to meet men downtown. In addition to the theaters, mainly the Paramount, there were department stores such as W.T. Grant, Harvey's, and Cain-Sloan, which had the larger men's room on the lower level and a smaller one on the top floor outside the Iris Room Restaurant. There was even a more private restroom on the second floor next to offices.

A very popular spot was in the lower-level restroom of the Noel Hotel at Fourth and Church Street. It had a side entrance with a half flight of steps that led down to a barber shop and a large men's room. The activity that took place there was staggering. There were usually six or seven stalls that were filled. By then, I had learned that men would move their foot toward the partition, just shy of coming into the next stall. Then they would tap their foot, to which the person in the adjoining stall, if interested, would respond in kind. Years later, I had a friend who, hilariously, compared that kind of scenario to tap dancing you might find in a Broadway show. I would often wonder what the barbers and their clientele thought of their front-row seat that allowed them to view the comings and goings in that men's room. I realize now that it was directly across the street from the Exchange Building where my dad worked for several years.

One block down from the Noel Hotel was the parking garage for Third National Bank. It had a lobby area with an elevator to the floor where your car had been parked. There was also a men's room, which was small and rarely used. The man who introduced me to this restroom was dressed in a three-piece, camel-colored herringbone suit, and looked every bit the attorney, which I learned years later had been his profession.

These assorted restrooms became my escape and refuge. They were places where I could be with men that had similar feelings. I did not have friends at church or school in whom I could confide and share my escapades. Boys like me could not be honest about their desires.

I was now 12, and my hormones were extreme. I had been exposed to sex with men, starting the first time I was molested at age 7. I knew what my wants were and felt ashamed that I was queer. Gay was not a term that I knew then. My desires had to be kept a secret. Boys my age and older would often call me "sissy" — to bully or make fun of me. I was at the age at which boys were noticing and talking about girls. But for me, instead of girls, I noticed boys. This gave me conflicted emotions and feelings of guilt. I had to be very careful that no one caught my glance when I would let it linger a little too long.

That was also the year that I came down with histoplasmosis, which is a type of lung infection, causing me to be out of school for three months. There were a couple of hospital stays and doctor's appointments, but most of that time was spent at home. My parents both worked, so I had a great deal of time alone. A "homebound teacher" stopped by three days a week to keep me current with my studies, thus allowing me to finish seventh grade in the spring of 1965.

With so much free time on my hands, I would often get bored and look for something to keep me entertained. Part of that was snooping through closets and drawers, leading me to try on some of my mother's clothes and then sing and dance in front of the full-length mirror in their bedroom. However, in the hall coat closet that my father used for his suits and overcoats, I discovered the real treasure. I found on the top shelf, tucked between two shoe boxes, a physique magazine. It was small, pocket-size, and the photos were in black and white. Physique magazines, popular from the 1930s through the 1960s, would show photos of young men, in various poses. They would often wear a small posing pouch that covered their genitals but left their backside nude. For me, this was the equivalent to what most other boys were feeling after finding their father's Playboy magazines.

I think back now and realize that I was so excited by my find that I never gave any thought as to why it was hidden in my dad's closet. For the next couple of months, I would look forward to any time alone that would allow me to sneak the magazine out carefully and stare at the photos. One day, my father came home early, and although I had time to hide the magazine in my room, there was not enough time to put it back in its original hiding place in his closet. I had to wait until the next day when he left for work to slide it back between the shoe boxes.

A few days later, I went to retrieve the magazine, and it was gone. It felt like my world had ended. I carefully took everything off the top shelf, just in case it had slipped behind the boxes. Did my dad realize that I had been looking at it? Or did my mother find the magazine and throw it out? Of course, my dad may have had second thoughts and decided he should not have brought it into our home.

I never asked him about it and feel confident that he would have denied having the magazine. Still, I knew it was there, and for a brief time, I felt okay being attracted to boys. It gave me a glimmer of hope, as I thought there must be other men who felt like me because there was a magazine showcasing male nudity.

Not long after the disappearance of the magazine, my mother bought my dad a subscription to Playboy, or that was the story my dad told me. The monthly issues would be kept under his bed, which makes me wonder now if that was done for my benefit. If he had known that I had been looking at his physique magazine, then he might have hoped an accessible Playboy would help spark an interest for me in girls.

Naturally, I looked at each issue, loved the cartoons, but could not have cared less about the photos of nude women. Then a new issue arrived with

an added feature: "Sex in Cinema." Its photos were geared heavily toward female actresses baring their all in movies, but much to my surprise, there were the occasional male counterparts showcased. The photos were smaller and did not compare to my earlier physique magazine experience, but at the moment it was all I had.

When I was in the eighth grade, my family stopped one day at the SupeRx drugstore near our home. The three of us entered the store and went in separate directions. While my parents did their shopping, I would look through the magazines. Even then, at age 13, I enjoyed looking at decorating magazines but would quickly place the magazine back on the rack if anyone was coming. Boys weren't supposed to like pretty things.

On the top shelf, partially covered by another magazine, I saw a physique pictorial. I had never seen one before on any magazine rack in any store, and it almost made me lightheaded. The how and why of this miracle escaped me, but it did not matter. This magazine was full-size, and in color, and the young blond surfer on the cover took my breath away. I had to have this magazine. I looked over the rack from top to bottom but did not see another copy. I knew my time was limited, and I also knew my parents would not buy it for me, even if I had mustered up the nerve to ask. The only solution I could think of was to tuck the magazine in the back of my shirt and hope I would not be stopped for shoplifting. To my amazement, I got it out of the store and home without an employee or my parents suspecting anything.

I immediately went to my room, flipped through the magazine, and then placed it between my mattress and box springs. This would be a temporary fix until I decided where to hide it. Eventually, I placed it behind the chest in my bedroom, where it lived for the next couple of years.

When my parents bought a larger home in 1968, I buried my magazine deep in a box of items from my room. I prayed that the movers would not drop or open the box before I had the chance to find a secure hiding spot. Fortunately, our new home had a huge walk-in attic where, between the rafters, under the insulation, I found my permanent hiding spot.

Until I began writing, I had not thought of that magazine for more than 40 years. I now realize that it could still be there. The next owner built additional rooms in the attic, which might mean that my now "vintage" physique magazine could be under the new flooring. Or it could have been a bit of a shock to the construction workers if they found it during the remodel.

Before I left for college, I was expected to be at church on Sunday mornings for Sunday School and worship service and then return that evening for Training Union and another worship service. On Wednesday evenings I would have choir practice or other activities. Our youth choir would take annual mission trips, which one summer brought us to New Orleans. With lots of free unchaperoned time to discover the city, I took a break and sat on a bench in Jackson Square. A nice young man sat down beside me. He told me that his name was Orlando, and I remember that he complimented me on my yellow shorts. Then he invited me to his home, and we walked the several blocks to what turned out to be a one-room walk-up. Although I was probably only 13 or 14 years old at the time, I had already become quite familiar with sex from the men at church, as well as from the downtown movie houses and department store restrooms. Following Orlando home did not make me as nervous as wondering if I would be able to retrace my steps back to rejoin our group.

During my pre-teen and teenage years, the church would often hold youth retreats at the Easter Seals facility located in an adjoining county. A guest preacher at one of those weekend retreats brought his son along with him. During that weekend the son, who was three years older than I, led me to a private area where we experimented. I did not share with him my stories of previous encounters with men in my church.

The last man from our church to seduce me came along when I was in my early teens. He learned my schedule and would often be waiting for me. His preferred rendezvous spot was the men's restroom, which was outside of the choir room next to the old sanctuary. From his wedding band, I knew he was married, but it would be years later that I would learn he had a son who, at age 30, was arrested on several counts of sexual battery for molesting young boys. Like father, like son.

It was also around this time that my first "official" girlfriend entered my life. Cindy was in the class ahead of me, and like 98 percent of the people I dated back then, she managed to earn my father's disapproval. I credit her for introducing me to Aretha Franklin's hit song *Respect*, and for educating me in the fine art of French kissing on a church-sponsored hayride. However, our relationship was doomed from the start. She lived in another area of town and attended another school, and, at 13, I was too young to drive. Our only time together was at church, and her parents, unlike mine, did not insist she be there every time the doors opened. I can now admit that I was probably a very needy boyfriend. By then, I had become accustomed to the special attention that I had received over the years from my male seducers.

It was during these early teenage years, at my father's insistence, that I joined a Boy Scouts troop. At the time, I did not know of the horrible mistake that he had made in Miami. Regardless, he felt Scouting was important, and I'm sure he hoped that it would make me more masculine. He would attend some of the meetings, and when I was away at camp, he would drive out for a visit. And a couple of times, he spent the night. I think now how those things would have alarmed my mother.

My dad had told me, after one of his overnight trips to see me at Boy Scouts camp, that he had done a tent check and found two boys "going at it" in their tent. The two boys were best of friends. I knew the boys through Scouting, but because they went to another school, I did not know them well. I also do not know if my father was telling the truth or if he just wanted to see my reaction. To this day, I'm not sure what his motive was in telling me, his 13-year-old son, something like that.

I had a close friend, David, who lived near me. We were in school together, and he had also joined the Scouts. He and I would share a tent on campouts and room together when we went away for two weeks to Boy Scouts camp. On one campout, I ended up sharing a tent with another of my classmates. During that overnight trip, my new friend wanted to mess around, and I

was more than willing. I assumed that this would be tame compared to things I had encountered during my summers downtown.

This was the first boy my age that I knew who seemed to have the same desires. He asked if I had ever let anyone "go down" on me. I lied and said, "No." He then proceeded to perform oral sex on me. I could barely contain myself and did not want it to end — and then he asked if I wanted to try. Many of the older men had asked the same of me, and although I had gotten more comfortable and had no problem using my hands, that was one thing I had yet to do. But with this beautiful boy gently guiding me, I was willing to do anything to please him. I don't think either of us got any sleep that night, but that did not matter. After dozens of sexual encounters with older men, this was different. It felt right and normal and appeared to be mutual. My young heart confused lust with love, and I fell hard.

Although we both attended Scouts and went to the same school, we did not have another opportunity to be together until summer. It was time for the annual two-week trek to camp, and I had already agreed to share the tent with my good friend, David. I wanted desperately, though, to be with the boy from the overnight campout, but that did not seem possible. The first week went as planned, but then temptation got the better of me. To this day, I can still see the hurt and confusion I caused when I told David that I was going to swap tents. He did not understand, and I could not tell him the real reason. Amazingly, he has reappeared in my life, and with no longer the need for secrets, I apologized and explained my reason for causing him hurt that summer long ago.

The last week of camp was everything I could have hoped for. Each night, I would crawl into my "boyfriend's" cot and fantasize that it could always be this way. In reality, I knew that this was impossible, and by the following summer he and his family had moved away. I had always held onto that "first love" feeling and tried to find him over the years. I was unsuccessful for quite some time, but eventually I located his older brother and reached out for contact.

I learned that he lives halfway across the country but still has a Nashville connection that brings him to town. On one of those visits, we met for coffee. It had been nearly 50 years, but still, I had butterflies and changed my outfit three times before going to see him. I don't know what I was expecting to happen, but I was not disappointed by our encounter. He has lived an amazing life, and I could not be happier for him.

When I confessed that I still had fond memories of our childhood encounters, I was prepared for this married childhood friend, who has children and grandchildren, to deny that anything had happened or to become upset with me. However, he said that he, too, remembered our time together fondly. It meant the world to me that he did not shatter the memory that I still hold precious, allowing me to continue thinking back to that time, that tent, that smile.

American politician and diplomat Howard Baker is credited for asking during the Watergate scandal, "What did the President know, and when did he know it?" I have asked myself the same question: What did I know about my father's tendencies, and when did I know it? Were there ever any signs that might have led me to question his actions?

At first, I would be quick to say no, but now I've had more time to reflect. Things that have not crossed my mind in decades now have me wondering why I never questioned them at the time — not just with my father, but with childhood friends and with my earlier sexual encounters.

In the 1950s and 1960s, I think many of these things were not talked about. "Respectable" people did not discuss sex. It was a time when television shows and movies often showed twin beds in the bedroom of a married couple. Then you add in a strict Southern Baptist upbringing during which heterosexual relationships were not discussed, and the thought of anything homosexual was completely forbidden and shocking. I was just a child and simply accepted things for what they were.

At the time, I'm sure that I did not fully understand. I wondered if it was wrong to have those feelings, or if I would be in trouble if I expressed them. Children's boundaries are not well-developed. The feelings that can be aroused by having sex with another person are powerful.

As I became older, but still before I could drive, my trips downtown became more limited. My parents thought that I would be fine alone at home, now that I had turned 14. I was, however, still expected to attend church on Wednesday nights and, in fact, enjoyed being there for choir practice. There were times that I would catch a ride with someone in the neighborhood but, one time, my father came home and picked me up.

I don't remember the excuse, probably school supplies, but one Wednesday I came up with some reason for him to drop me off at W.T. Grant's, saying that I would then walk the three blocks to church. I breezed through the front door of Grant's, and then down the escalator and out the side door on the lower level. There was a walkway that led to Cain-Sloan department store's lower level, where a very active men's room was located. I never asked, but I assume that my dad was crossing through the intersection when he saw me darting out of the side door, away from where I had told him I needed to be.

The stalls in the men's room were lined opposite from the door you entered. Peeking between the stall door and partition, you could view the person entering the restroom. I had been doing precisely that when I saw my dad walk in. He stood there for a moment, most likely looking at the shoes and pants shown by each man below the stall door, and then turned and walked out.

How was this possible? And more importantly, what was I to do now? Although I hoped he had gone on, my fear was that he would be waiting outside of the restroom for me. As I suspected, he was standing there and simply said, "Let's go." Nothing more was said on the way to the car or on the short drive to church. He knew why I was there and what I was doing or had planned to do, and yet he had nothing to say.

How did he know where I would be? Why did he assume, that in that vast, three-story department store, I would be in the lower level men's room? I can understand his suspicions. I had told him one thing, but then he saw me going elsewhere. This also meant that he would have to have known about that men's room being an active hookup place, to assume I would go directly there.

Even though we never discussed it, I have to think that my actions that day would have confirmed for him that I was a homosexual, which I now know is something he was more familiar with than he ever let on.

I found a photo album from when my dad was Scoutmaster. My father was an amateur photographer and, until our last residence, always had a darkroom in our home. I imagine that the photos in that album were taken by my father and were developed in his private darkroom. Many of the photos were of the Boy Scouts swimming at Snapper Creek in Florida. All of that would have been very innocent, except the boys were nude. Because of the time period, late 1940s-1950s, that may not have been unusual. I remember, when I was a child, my dad dropping me off at the Nashville downtown YMCA, long before the facilities became co-ed. At that time, the facility's indoor pool was clothing-optional.

Discovering this photo album again, after my dad's passing, made me fearful of it being viewed as child pornography. I mentioned it to Ronald Berdeaux, the only remaining Boy Scout I knew from my dad's troop, and ended up mailing it to him. When I was born, he was a 13-year-old Boy Scout. My contact with him through the years was from birthday and Christmas cards, reminding me that I was named Ronald after him. Yes, I was named after a 13-year-old Boy Scout, who I learned later was not only gay but had been arrested in 1985 for sexually abusing a minor. He has since died, which leaves me to wonder where that photo album might be now.

Going through the stacks of papers and envelopes, where I had scribbled lyrics to long-forgotten melodies during this period of teen angst, I found most are embarrassing and amateurish. However, as I read through them now, I realize how badly I was trying to express my feelings through song. One song in particular I wrote for my parents in 1968. Of course, I never had the courage to share it with them.

When I was young, I followed in your steps.
Is that why you blame yourselves for my mistakes?
Don't put your labels on me,
I am what I choose to be.
Don't put your labels on me,
Oh no, let me be free.
You taught me how to live day to day,
But now, I'm old enough, I'll go my own way.
You taught me right from wrong, and how to be strong,
You taught me how to share, you taught me how to care,
And now, I give you love and hope you'll see,
Although a part of you, I still must be me.

FOUR

RISKY BUSINESS

AGES 15-17

We moved to a larger home when I was 15. It was in the same Nashville neighborhood of West Meade and had been custom built by Bill and Nita Payne, who were also members of our church. They had owned a pair of clothing stores in the area, and we had developed a friendship over the years through shopping with them. The husband, Bill, ran the men's store, and one block down, Nita operated the women's store. Bill would often have sample clothing, and there was a time that I could fit into a sample size. I remember being so excited when he gave me a pair of hip-hugging bell-bottom pants. Although these pants were rarely a good look for anyone, for a brief moment I felt very much in vogue.

When Bill died suddenly of a heart attack, we became even closer to Nita. She was wonderful, outspoken and daring in an "Auntie Mame" sort of way. I bonded with her, and she saw me for who I was, although we never

discussed my sexuality. The first time I went to their home, my parent's and I were out delivering Christmas presents. I climbed the steps to the wide front porch, lined with rocking chairs, and rang the doorbell. Nita opened the door, and I saw before me a grand entrance hall with a black-and-white tile floor. It made such an impression on me that years later I created a black-and-white checked logo for my design business. And to this day, I still incorporate black-and-white checks, or black-and-white piano keys, into my artwork.

Eventually, Nita realized the home was larger than she needed and the vast hillside lot required more upkeep and time than she was willing to give. She decided she wanted to scale down, sell the house, and she wanted us to buy it. I'm not sure about all of the wheeling and dealing that went on, but she made my dad an incredible offer, complete with owner financing. In the spring of my sophomore year we moved, and although I was only 15, my parents allowed me to drive the family station wagon, filled with boxes, the short distance to the new house.

Nita moved into a brand-new apartment complex, where my dad dropped me off so that I could help her unpack. Her hair stylist had also been recruited to help. Nita's hair was never out of place, and this was the man responsible. She said she thought we might have a lot in common and wanted us to meet. It turned out that we did have a lot in common. We both liked men. I was 15, and he was probably 10 years older, or more. Nita had just set us up!

Once she saw the connection, she said she was tired and needed to rest. She asked her friend if he'd mind running me home, adding that my parents weren't expecting me anytime soon, so maybe I could go home with him for a bit.

He lived in a two-story apartment building that looked like it had been a 1950s Holiday Inn in a former life. There was a balcony walkway that circled the building with one door opening into his living area and another door, on the back, that opened into his bedroom. Once we were there, clothes came off, and if there had been a chandelier, I would have expected him to swing from it. It was an educational and very energetic afternoon. My previous experiences had taken place in confined church classrooms, public restrooms or tents, so this allowed a level of freedom and privacy I had not known.

Eventually, Nita called and said it was time to take me home. However, she felt it would be best if he returned me to her place so that she could take me. I'm sure she did not want to alarm my parents. Plus, this kept the hair stylist totally off their radar.

I continued to see him when we were able to work out a plan. Eventually, when I turned 16 and had my driver's license, I had many more opportunities for a tryst when my parents would let me borrow one of their cars. Nita called me one day to say the Antique Fair was coming up and wondered if I'd like to go with her. Of course: one) just to be with her, and two) antiques. What's not to love? She picked me up from school, and I assumed we were headed to the antique show, but she had other plans. She drove us to the Buick dealership, saying she needed to talk with someone.

In the late 1960s, our local Buick dealership marketed the German import, Opel Kadett. This little sportster was top of my list of favorite cars. At the dealership, she got out and asked me to join her. I gladly hopped out of the car and walked with her and the salesman through a sea of new cars. She stopped in front of a tan, brand-new 1969 Opel with black vinyl roof and asked what I thought about it. I told her I loved it and confessed, as if she did not already know, that it was my dream car. With that, she handed me a set of car keys and said, "It's yours." I was speechless. It had to be a cruel joke. But no, she had already purchased the car for me and simply told me to be careful driving it home. I begged her to follow me, but she declined, saying that it was my surprise to share.

I drove home carefully, and once I turned onto our street I ended up behind my mother's car. She was coming home from work and did not realize I was behind her until she started up the driveway, and I began honking the horn. By the time we had reached the top, my dad had come out to see what was all of the commotion. Nita had not let them in on the surprise.

My father was furious. I don't know if it was because he could not afford to buy me a car or because he thought I was too young to own a car, but tensions ran high as he called her. Whatever she said calmed him, and

Ron and his Dad's shadow and new car

knowing her, I'm sure he realized that she would not back down, so he might as well accept it.

Nita never asked me anything about the connection she had made for me with her hair stylist. I am not sure if he had confided in her or not. In fact, the only time she said anything remotely about my sexuality came several years later, when I became engaged during my junior year of college. As I told her the exciting news, she replied by asking if I was sure — 100 percent sure — that was what I wanted.

When I had my driver's license, I began dating Donna, another one of my church friends. She lived on the other side of town, and although my father worried about his 16-year-old son driving late at night, at least she met

Ron with prom date, Donna, 1969

with his approval. Two of my friends from church, who attended high school with me and lived in our neighborhood, were also dating girls from our church that lived across town. The three of us asked the three of them to our high school prom — my first and last triple date. All I seem to remember from that night is the six of us in formal attire trying to fit into my parents' car.

It was on my way home after a high school date with Donna that I picked up a young man who turned out to be a hustler. My route home would lead me through downtown Nashville, and in the late 1960s the Lower Broad area was quite seedy. As I stopped at a red light, I looked to my right and saw an attractive young man staring at me. He smiled, nodded and started walking toward my car. I felt a flash of panic, mixed with excitement. He tapped on the passenger side window indicating for me to roll it down. The light changed, and the car behind me honked, so he motioned for me to pull over into one of the metered parking spaces. I should have driven on, but I was intrigued.

Once I was parked, with the engine still running, he opened the side door and sat down. I was startled by his forwardness, and yet as a horny 16-year-old, I was curious as to where this was going. We made small talk for a bit as his hand rested on my thigh. He then asked if I had some place to go where we could be alone. I still cringe from my reckless decision. We were parked at Fourth and Broad. Three blocks up on the left, at Seventh and Broad, was First Baptist Church. And I had a key. My father was in charge of the sound system in the sanctuary, and I would sometimes assist him. Because of this responsibility, I had keys to the building. This was 1969 — a time before alarm systems, cameras, security and such.

It was a few minutes past 11 p.m. My curfew was midnight. If anything was going to happen, it needed to happen now. I drove us to the parking lot on the backside of the church. We got out, and I unlocked the church door. For some reason, I felt more comfortable leading my new friend up three flights of stairs, to the Intermediate Department, where in the back classroom I had attended Sunday School — and where my father served as superintendent of the department. We did not need to turn on a light, as the moon was full and illuminated the room through the windows. This felt familiar and yet at the same time different as we undressed. However, this was only the third time for me to have sexual relations with someone close to my own age. As much as I hate to admit it, there was the added excitement that came from the danger and the fear of being caught. And yet I was comfortable having sex in my church. After all, it had started nine years earlier, through no fault of my own.

As we were getting dressed again, my new friend said he usually charged $20. I wasn't sure what he meant, and seeing the confusion on my face, he asked, "You didn't think this was free, did you?" All of a sudden it sank in. I thought back on all of the times I had been offered money by my seducers. I would feel offended and always turned it down. But now, I realized paying for sex was a reality. But it was the other reality that really frightened me. I did not have twenty dollars.

Recovering quickly, I said, "Sure," then added that I needed to go to the restroom first. I started walking toward the hall, hoping he would wait, but instead he followed. We went into the men's room, where I stepped up to the urinal while he went into a stall. Once he began to urinate, I ran as fast as I could out the door, down three flights of stairs and fumbled to unlock my car door. I was in my car and starting to back out of the parking space when he came bounding out of the church door. The car was moving as he unsuccessfully tried to open the locked passenger door, but as I pulled into the street he kicked the side of the car, which I discovered later, left a noticeable dent.

My heart was racing, and I knew it would be after curfew before I got home. I also knew my father would be sitting in his chair waiting for me, as he always did when I went out. The unknown was wondering what kind of punishment he would have planned for me. This was long before cellphones, so other than stopping at a pay phone, delaying my arrival even more, I had no choice but to keep driving and arrived 20 minutes late.

I ended up being grounded for two weeks — and when he questioned me the next morning about the dent in my car, I lied. In spite of how that night ended, I was left with an unforgettable experience and absolutely no one that I could share it with.

Before I was given a car, I would beg to borrow either my dad's Chrysler station wagon or, preferably, my mother's yellow Cadillac Sedan DeVille. She loved that car with its soft yellow exterior and yellow cloth seats trimmed in matching leather. However, as much as I enjoyed driving her car, I have one Cadillac-related teenage memory that still haunts me.

Friends were few in high school, with chorus being the only class where I seemed to excel. I often had a lead role in the annual musical productions, such as Marryin' Sam in *Li'l Abner*. It was also one of the few classes that included students from several grades. This broadened my chance of finding friends, which in turn allowed me to become close with several girls in the class behind me. The fact that I had my driver's license did not hurt. The relationships were not romantic, but I was more like the token "gay best friend," long before that term became popular, long before I admitted my sexual orientation.

I did have a couple of friends in chorus who were boys. Dennis was my age, and my other friend was a year younger. I developed such a crush on the younger one and would sometimes find myself crossing the line with my words or actions, then quickly laugh and insist I was kidding. Dennis and I were not that close, but we did have some interesting conversations. He felt every bit the outcast, as I did, once we were outside of the chorus classroom.

One conversation Dennis and I had concerned one of our male teachers. The man was not classically handsome, plus he had an arrogant air of someone overly confident. For me, that only added to his sexiness. Or maybe it was the fact that he wore the tightest pants of any of the faculty. He would prop himself against his desk, proudly displaying his bulge at the eye level of students seated in front of him. Neither Dennis or I admitted to each other that we felt an attraction. Plus, we were not the only ones gossiping about him. He was talked about for many reasons, the most popular subject being the well-known affair that this married man was having with a female student.

One day Dennis told me he had heard this teacher liked to walk around nude at home. I asked how he knew that. He would not say who had mentioned it but said they knew because they had looked in his windows at night. True or not, this made me very curious and excited me to the point that I wanted to see for myself. So one evening while my parents were out with friends, I picked up Dennis, and we went by our teacher's home. He lived in our neighborhood, closer to Dennis than me. I parked my mother's Caddy across the street and a couple of houses down. We carefully walked in the dark up his driveway and behind his home. All of the drapes were pulled tight, with just a sliver of light coming through. I was disappointed until I saw the uncovered window in his garage. Being just a one-car garage, the exterior window was not more than 12 feet from the door leading into the house. That door had an uncovered window on the top half, but from our position we were still unable to see into the house.

Dennis then noticed the exterior garage window was not locked and started to push it upward. He dared me to crawl through the window and go over to the door leading into the house and take a look. We had come this far, so I really did not need much coaxing. Once inside the garage, I quietly approached the interior door and just as I looked in, his wife noticed my movement and screamed. With just a quick glimpse of my teacher, I turned and jumped back through the window.

Dennis had taken off running. I was so rattled that instead of jumping in my car and driving away, I also ran. Once I realized my mistake, I knew it was too late to turn back, so I kept running. It did not take long for the police to pick me up and take me to the station. My parents, along with their friends, were at a play downtown. The police met them at the theater and asked them to come with them to where I was being held.

Fortunately, my teacher did not press charges on the condition that I receive professional help. I never told the police that I had a friend with me that night. I was the one who foolishly entered their garage, not Dennis. My parents were understandably horrified by my actions and especially embarrassed that it happened while they were with friends. I had no words to say, or none that I thought they would want to hear, to explain my behavior. Unable to look them in the eyes, I waited for them to yell at me, but they too were speechless. We rode home in silence as tears streamed down my mother's face.

My father drove me to my therapy appointments, with very little conversation. I finally confessed that I had not been not alone that night and that I had entered the garage on a dare. Of course, that still did not justify my actions. I had four sessions with the child psychiatrist and remember becoming defensive, almost to the point of being hostile, when he told me during the first session that I could be cured from my unnatural attraction to boys. I was 16 years old and had always felt that way. It was then that I decided that I would listen to his nonsense, nod, and say what he wanted to hear. I knew who and what I was, but made the conscious decision to play whatever game was needed to get the hell away from this man. I was so used to lying to cover up or explain my behavior that I had no problem doing so with this man.

In school, I was transferred into another class for the remainder of the year. I assumed many of the faculty knew the reason why. Fortunately, with students being so self-absorbed, hardly anyone noticed. Dennis was relieved and grateful that I kept him out of it, but our friendship changed. I still wonder, how did he really know our teacher enjoyed being naked at home? Did someone tell him, like he said, or had he been the one looking in their windows? I think I knew he had the same feelings as I did, and yet we never talked about our attraction to men.

I have kept my school annuals from seventh through 12th grade. Each year, we would all scramble to have as many friends and teachers sign our books. I found in my sophomore annual an inscription from Dennis saying: "It's been a wonderful year, hasn't it? It has for me. And thanks for helping make my first year at Hillwood a very pleasant one."

I had not realized, or maybe I just forgot, that Dennis did not sign my annual the following year — our junior year. Of course, after the incident at our teacher's home, I had kept my distance. However, as I flipped through my senior annual, I found:

"Number 1! (as usual) Well, it sure has been a fantabulous year, hasn't it?

Wow, meeting so many new people, getting to know the old ones better ... It's been real fun, I must admit. In fact, it's been my best year yet! The last one is supposed to be, I guess, and of course it is. I sure will remember all of the sneaky things we did together. ... Maybe, when we're old and gray, we can call the gang together and meet. ... As always, Dennis"

I wish that I could live the way I want to,
Not worry about others or have them worry about me.
To escape from the world and all its faults,
And be left alone with just my dreams and memories.

I had reached my breaking point. Church = Sex. Movies = Sex. Restrooms = Sex. Scouts = Sex.

The attention I craved as a child had now become an addiction, with the need for each hit to be bigger than the one before. I thought of the hours that I had spent in the downtown restrooms waiting for someone to want me. I thought about the family friend who, when I was 15 years old, set me up with her hairstylist. I thought about the physique magazines that had given me a thrill. And I thought about the fellow Boy Scout and how I equated sex with love. And the boy in chorus — the one I desperately wanted to feel as I did — who saw me break down in unexplained tears one afternoon, as I drove him home from school — I just wanted him to hold me. I thought about the night I picked up a hustler and what transpired within my Sunday School classroom, and I thought about the preacher's son at the youth retreat — the church choir trip to New Orleans and how I blindly followed a young man to his apartment. And then I thought about the night I crawled through that teacher's window, the scream, the police, my parent's confusion and, most of all, their disappointment.

All of this came crashing down on me during a time my parents had gone away for the weekend. I could no longer see my life having any value. There was no one that I felt I could talk to, and I was too embarrassed to do so, even if there were. I kept asking myself, why did I find pleasure in what the rest of the world saw as wrong, sick, deviant? The boys who called me queer and sissy were right. Even they could see me for what I was.

This had to end. I did not have access to a gun or pills. I thought about taping the cracks around the garage door and placing towels on the floor against the bottom of the doors so nothing would escape — and with the car full of gas, I would start the engine. I did not know how long it would take for me to succumb to the fumes. I wished there was something that I could take to knock me out first so that I could sleep as the poisonous air ended my life. But I feared, with our garage near the next door neighbor's bedroom window, that they might hear the engine running through the night and alert someone.

I moved on from that idea to choosing a sharp knife from the kitchen drawer and trying to cut my wrist. There was no internet for me to Google and find the quickest way to draw blood. I tried and tried but only found the courage to make superficial cuts. Yes, there was blood, lots of blood, but nothing that would end my life immediately.

My thoughts were filled with concern for the pain that I would, once again, cause my parents. And the mess, the awful mess they would come home to. As my hysterical crying became calmer, I placed a paper towel against my wrist to stop the bleeding. Once that was under control, I began to wipe the blood from the kitchen floor. I gathered the bloody paper towels, put them in a bag, then placed the bag in the outside trash can. I tried to hide them under the newspapers and garbage already in the can. Then I washed my arm and used several Band-Aids to cover the scratches and cuts I had made in my desperation.

It was spring and the days were warm, but I wore a long-sleeved shirt to make sure my bandaged arm was hidden when my parents returned Sunday evening from their brief trip. My mother began to unpack while my dad sat in his favorite chair, opened the Sunday paper and began to read. I was in bed by the time he had finished and placed the newspaper in the trashcan. I must have left some trace of the bloody towels, because for whatever reason, something caused him to dig deeper and find what I had hoped would never have been seen. My mother came into my room and sat on the edge of my bed. Her beautiful face showed the pain and worry that, once again, I had caused. She looked at my arm to make sure I had stopped the bleeding. I confessed that I had thought their lives would be better if I was gone. She held me for the longest time, and as we cried together, she assured me of her endless love.

I have no idea of my parent's conversation that evening, as I was physically and mentally exhausted and drifted off to sleep. I did not go to school for a few days, letting my arm begin to heal. When I returned to school, I had a note to excuse me from gym. I did not want to be changing in a locker room and putting on a T-shirt for class. Within a week, the scratches were practically healed, and one Band-Aid covered the deepest of the cuts.

Although my parents and I talked, I never said I was queer. I never said I had been molested for the past 10 years, or that I had reached a point of begging for the attention that was described as abnormal. I was just a teenager going through the stress all teenagers go through, and I would survive. It would get better. But as an adult, I now know that my parents were not blind. They read between the lines that I spoke. They just did not know how to respond.

Was I changed by my actions? Did I want to live? Did I think of trying it again? Let me just say that no, there was not a miraculous revelation. I did not feel changed and, yes, I thought about suicide again. I felt every bit as alone as before the attempt. I still had no one in my life to talk with or be honest about what I was feeling. Once again, I simply put on my smiling facade and made the best of things. But inside, deep inside, I still hurt. I was still confused, lonely and continued to seek anonymous sexual encounters, hoping to provide a few brief moments of feeling normal. Or what had become normal for me.

After graduation, I went to college. I lost touch with my friend Dennis and had no idea where he ended up, or what he did after high school. I regret that I dropped him from my life. He was a reminder of that night, the night I crossed the imaginary line and could not find my way back. The night that resulted in my world exploding. I would not let myself think about him. I focused on an entirely new set of issues — college.

Then, one day, I heard that Dennis had succeeded where I had failed. Two years after graduation, I was told Dennis had committed suicide.

I've tried to make it on my own,
But Lord, you know that I'm not strong.
So Lord, I beg, please let tomorrow come.

♫

I have read that actors have said they won't do a nude scene in a movie unless it is integral to the plot. At this point, I feel that I am in the middle of my own nude scene. I am naked but also feel that it is integral to my story. No more hiding or covering up. I have exposed myself through my confessions, and although I know some might prefer to look away, I hope others will see hope and not turn their backs.

My life is filled with contradictions. From birth until I was in my late 40s, my world revolved around church and religion. My mother was a church secretary until my birth. My dad was Scoutmaster for a troop sponsored by the church. When his crime was revealed and he was placed in jail awaiting trial, my mother returned to the church as a part-time employee to make ends meet. While separated, her letters to him spoke of attending various services and events connected to the church. His letters to her spoke of wishing the "preacher" would come to see him, and requesting she bring a New Testament to him in jail. Once that was done, his letters began to include Scriptures that he found comfort in through that difficult time. And when the trial was over and he followed a job out of state, he would write to my mother and tell her about the church or revival he had attended, while she and I were left in Miami trying to sell our home.

In 1956, our family reunited in Nashville, Tennessee and found a church home at First Baptist. My mother took a job with the Christian Life Commission and each year would attend the Southern Baptist Convention. My dad became a church deacon and eventually a Trustee with the Baptist Sunday School Board. After high school, I went on to attend a Southern

Baptist college, and I worked as a part-time music director in two Baptist churches for a period of 10 years.

As a family, we would attend Sunday morning and evening services as well as the Wednesday night services and various activities such as choir or church retreats. Our life revolved around the church. No one in Tennessee, including me, knew about my dad's arrest for molesting a minor in the church's Boy Scouts troop. Nor did anyone know about my years of being sexually abused within the classrooms, restrooms, church retreats and even on a youth choir trip associated with First Baptist church.

I have asked myself, why me? In my mother's letters are little anecdotes she shared with my dad about my behavior at ages 2 and 3. Reading them, I realized they seem to confirm, to me at least, what I have always known. I am gay. And even though I know better, I can't help but wonder if my behavior was a result of being alone with my mother for nearly six months at such a young age? Wearing her high-heeled shoes, or jewelry, insisting my pillowcases have embroidered flowers like hers, were early signs that carried into my adult years. A friend from church, a few years older than me and also gay, recently confided that he and one of his church mates as teenagers would talk about me, thinking and predicting that I was queer. Of course, what they did not know was their prediction had come true. I was already being used for sexual gratification by men within our church.

I knew my father loved me, and I would hear from others that he was proud and would often brag about me. Still, I felt a distance, a disconnect, a feeling that I might have been a disappointment to him. We seemed to have so little in common. My likes were much more in tune with my mother than my dad. I will never know for sure, but I have wondered if the distance I felt was intentional on his part because of the past accusations of pedophilia. I did not know about his crime then. Now that I do, I realize those thoughts would have been something he lived with daily. There also might have been fear or concerns from my mother, or a feeling that she was closely watching his actions.

In the spring of 1969, my parents' friends from church were in need of a house sitter. They had a spacious home, filled with antiques, and they were going to be out of town for a few days. Somehow, I got the job. I'm sure they never expected that I would flirt with a sales clerk at a nearby department store and invite him over after he got off work. We made a date, and I gave him our church friends' address. A few minutes before he was to arrive, I opened the front door and sat on the porch steps. I was there as he drove up, anxious for what was about to happen. Once again, it never dawned on me that I was taking a risk.

And although I had fun, it was his comment on the way out that still echoes in my memory. He said that seeing me sitting on the steps, waiting for him, almost made him drive away, thinking that I appeared to be so desperate.

I was still 16 when I started my senior year of high school. Fortunately, it was uneventful as I tried to stay low-key and off everyone's radar. Chorus was still my most successful subject, and I had a good relationship with my teacher. The music room was in one of the portable classrooms, in front of the school, detached from the main building. My teacher arranged for me to take my study hall period in that room, since there was not a class that met during that time. I would sometimes study, often sit and play the piano, and when my teacher was away, jump in my car and leave campus for lunch. That was a huge no-no, but I got away with it quite often.

I would skip school, more than I should have, to simply ride around neighborhoods and downtown. One day, in Centennial Park, I kept circling the Parthenon until I found the courage to park and walk over to speak with a young man in a sailor uniform sitting on a picnic table. We chatted about nothing for a while until he mentioned how much he would love to take a long, hot shower. Warning lights should have flashed in my head, but knowing my parents were at work, I took him home with me. I turned on the water while he undressed, and when his clothes were piled on the floor he turned to me and began to unbutton my shirt. I let him undress me and pull me into the hot shower.

So many things could have gone wrong that day. A 16-year-old skipping school, picking up a stranger and taking him to his family home while his parents were at work. Dangerous on so many levels. And yet while my classmates were dealing with geometry and Latin, I was doing my patriotic duty by soaping up a sailor in my dad's shower. I also was learning to cover my tracks better, as I remembered to put the wet towels in the dryer and wipe down the bathroom before driving my paramour back to the park.

When I would skip school, I would forge my mother's signature on the note that I would turn in the following day. I did that so often that it raised suspicion in the office. The staff began to compare notes that had been kept on file over the years. The handwriting did not match, and so one day they called my mom to discuss my absenteeism. She confirmed she had written the note regarding my reason for missing the previous day. Of course, that was not the truth, but she did not want me to get into any more trouble with the school. However, when I got home, it was totally different, and the hammer came down hard on me for missing school and forging her signature. Still, I think that, after the drama from the previous year, my parents proceeded with caution in disciplining me.

The musical that year was *Annie Get Your Gun*, and while I did not secure the lead role, I still had a good supporting part that included two duets. My dad, the amateur photographer, had taken many photos the previous year, but I have only found a few pictures from this production.

In the spring, the school held its annual Senior Variety Show. My *Annie Get Your Gun* co-star and I had practiced a duet to perform that night, but she had to back out. I was very fortunate that one of my fellow chorus students came to my rescue. I had found what I thought to be a very fashionable

outfit to wear, and my singing partner borrowed an outfit my from mother that complemented. I thought we rocked the house, musically and stylishly.

I had a second performance that night of an original composition. I sat at the grand piano, with a glittered sign off to one side that said *Originals by JRMY*. My full name is James Ronald Monnie York, and my initials create the unfortunate nickname that kids would pronounced as "Germy." But still, at age 17, I had my moment of glory when I sang:

> *Thru the clouds, I can see the sun,*
> *In spite of the rain coming down.*
> *And the lightning is all around,*
> *The darkness seems to overcome,*
> *But I see the sun.*

Graduation finally arrived, and in spite of everyone's concern I did receive my diploma. But as I walked up to the platform, the principal mispronounced my name. JAMES. RONALD. MONNIE, which he pronounced as *Moan-y*, YORK. It did not matter, I had graduated in the Class of 1970.

Several classmates ended up at the same college as me. My sophomore class music teacher and I would cross paths occasionally, as she had entered the field of real estate. My junior/senior class music teacher gave me an eyeful when I would run into him at a local health club, where I learned first hand of his notorious reputation for getting a bit grabby in the whirlpool and steam room. But as far as high school, I left it in the rear-view mirror.

I was invited to work on the 10-year reunion planning committee. I agreed to help but panicked when pulling up for the first meeting at the home of one of my fellow students. The bad memories from high school overshadowed the good, and I felt like driving away. The home was lovely, and all of the cars in the drive seemed nicer than mine. I felt inadequate, a failure. And yet, in reality, I was none of those. I gathered up my nerve and rang the doorbell. Everyone was so nice and appreciative of me wanting to help.

Because of that, I enjoyed the 10-year reunion as well as the one after that. I missed the next two reunions, one of which happened about the time of my father's sudden death. I was overwhelmed and not feeling sociable. However, I was back on the planning committee for the 40th reunion and again for the 45th. Our committee had shrunk, but then, so had our class. This is why we opted to reconnect every five years now instead of 10. Those that may have been just acquaintances in the past are now dear friends and a part of my life. Cliques and pretenses have gone away as we have aged. I can now look back on high school and see some good.

I'M SATISFIED

I'm satisfied, I'm satisfied,
With the good and the bad in my life.
'Cause I know, whether right or wrong,
It's not the singer, oh no, it's the song.

When I was young, and oh, so foolish,
I always wanted, what I couldn't have.
But now I know, and you'll have to agree,
There's a difference between want, and need.

And I've tried, and sometimes failed,
Sometimes Heaven, and sometimes Hell.
But I know, I'm satisfied,
'cause I know, down in my soul,
At least I tried.
And that makes me satisfied.

F I V E

College Dreams

AGE 18 +

I applied to two Baptist-affiliated colleges, Samford University in Birmingham and Belmont University in my hometown of Nashville. My parents, especially my father, felt strongly about me staying close to home. I am sure he was pleased when I found myself on the waiting list for Samford and, thus, Belmont bound.

As an only child, my parents and I decided I would opt for a single dorm room for my freshman year. I think we all hoped I would find a friend to share a room the following year, and actually I did. I bonded with the boy in the room next to mine, "Gary." He was from Kentucky and the son of a preacher. Belmont had a great deal of preacher kids enrolled.

I look back now and can clearly see my patterns in relationships. If a boy became my friend, I would often mistake friendship for more. And so it

College Bound

began. I wanted to be with him as much as possible. We only had a couple of classes together, but as lowly freshmen we had a lot in common. One holiday, he came home with me for the weekend. I wanted to share my room, my bed, with him, but my parents had the guest room ready. Things would have been very awkward if I insisted on any other arrangement.

As our friendship grew, we decided to be roommates our sophomore year. We were assigned one of the larger, quieter rooms in a back corner. Unfortunately, he backed out of school just before the semester began. His family wanted him closer to home and at a more affordable state school. Because he made such a last-minute withdrawal, I was still given the double room but not a replacement roommate.

During our first year together at Belmont, I wrote a song that only he knew was written for him. The title is *Dreamin' of Things to Come,* because he kept reminding me to live in the present and not worry or plan what will happen in the future. One of my friends, who I sang with in the school's chorale, liked my song and would often perform it at a choir concert as well as around town.

My Kentucky friend and I kept in touch the following year, and I drove to Lexington one weekend to visit him. He had a small apartment that I could not help but imagine what it would be like to share with him. He had asked me earlier in the day to smoke a joint with him. I declined because, as a vocal major, I felt smoking could be harmful to my voice. I knew my answer had disappointed him and also knew smoking one joint would have not done any damage. And yet, for some reason, I stuck by my answer.

During that weekend, our relationship changed. I confessed my feelings and how I coveted more. After I had confided that I was sexually attracted to him, "Gary" offered a proposal. If I would smoke a joint with him, then he would experiment sexually with me. I knew he was heterosexual but had hoped to convince him there were other options. He was willing to be with me sexually because he cared for me, maybe loved me in his own way.

It was a perfect afternoon as we laid in each other's arms on his mattress on the floor. We laughed at the awkwardness but still proceeded onward. For me, it was magical. For him, it was a one-time gift. What I did not know at the time was that it was also a goodbye gift. On my drive back to Nashville, my head was filled with thoughts of moving in with him, and our life together. Once I was back in Nashville, we talked by phone a few more times, but it was not the same. I had lost him because I wanted more from him than he was able to give. This became the pattern for all of my male relationships. And yet it did not stop me from *"Dreamin' of things to come."*

DREAMIN' OF THINGS TO COME

In the morning, I face, a lonely heart in an empty place,
Without you, I'm dreamin', I'm dreaming of things to come.

And at noon, when I phone, it's the same old story, nobody's home,
I'm without you, but I'm dreamin', I'm dreamin' of things to come.

You always told me, never plan tomorrow, till it comes.
Now I know why, cause tomorrow's here, and, you are gone.

But I still wait, in the evening, listening for your footsteps,
To tell me, you're coming, you're coming home to me.

I have many wonderful memories from my time at Belmont, and I made lifelong friends. I would venture to say campus life today is much different than my time there in the early 1970s. Boys did not have a curfew, while girls had to be in their dorms by 10 p.m. In fact, girls were not allowed to wear pants to the cafeteria on Sundays. The restrictions imposed on the girls, along with the total lack of restrictions for boys, made some want to take risks and break rules. Many of the students had not been away from home before and found this freedom intoxicating.

Students were required to take courses in Bible and attend an hour-long Chapel service twice a week. Homosexual behavior was not tolerated, and yet it was rampant. One of the more flamboyant students, Larry, was eventually asked to leave school. I had avoided him on campus as I tried to keep a low profile. However, by my senior year we had become best friends and eventually roommates for several years. At one point, he even worked for my father. The most startling connection, though, was finding out that he was the nephew of my parents' lifelong friends, one of whom was also my mother's former boss, from their days in Miami. (Friends that I now know were close during the time of my father's arrest.)

There were so many questionable things that happened on this Southern Baptist campus that those in charge were either unaware of or had turned a blind eye. One of the male dormitory resident assistants was a closeted gay man who began an affair with a music student in the class behind me. Eventually, that student spent more nights in the RA's room than his own dorm room. A female teacher in the drama department became quite the talk around campus as rumors flew about a preacher's wife leaving her husband to move in with her. And to this day, they still live together, more than 40 years later. These things were scandalous in the 1970s.

There was a male student who, in hopes of a sexual encounter, would knock on my dorm room at night. This would end in his overwhelming guilt, causing him to become angry and declare it would never happen again. However, the next evening, knock, knock, knock — and the cycle would continue. My future roommate, Larry, had many similar experiences before leaving school.

Girls, because of their curfew restrictions, could be found crawling in and out of their first-floor dorm windows and having a friend sign their name on the check-in list, as if they had returned and were safe and sound in their room.

I had a few dates with girls during my time at Belmont. But there were two where the relationship became more serious. One lived in the dorm next to mine. We had fun together our freshman year, and I often would spend time with her, her roommate and a couple of other girlfriends in her dorm. One evening several of us piled into my car and headed to the theater to see the just-released blockbuster *Love Story*. Being forewarned that it was a tearjerker, the girls brought rolls of toilet paper instead of Kleenex. Again, I look back and think of myself as the "gay best friend," but in the world of a Southern Baptist campus, I could not be gay. So we continued to date, and I even went to Louisiana to meet her family.

Dating was fun, but then came the required kissing and such. I was fine with kissing, but in the often-deserted "dating parlors" located in Belmont's historical mansion, I experienced her need for more. I wanted to make her happy and, honestly, I wanted to keep suspicions about my sexuality at bay. But as wonderful and lovely as she was, I felt so uncomfortable when she would place my hand on her bare breasts, expecting more.

Eventually we broke up. She had been wary of me from the beginning because I spent a great deal of my freshman year with Jane, who lived in the other dorm. My girlfriend had misinterpreted the relationship as romantic but, in truth, we were just good friends, and lonely. We attended church together, and she was in love with Phil, one of my closest male friends from church and high school, as well as part of my prom triple date.

Since so much of my time was spent in the music department, I developed a friendship in my sophomore year with Carol, a fellow music student. She was in a toxic relationship, and I became her confidant. Once again, I was the "gay best friend" without admitting to being homosexual. Our friendship grew, and I fell in love with her. Eventually, she broke off her engagement, something that needed to be done, but then transferred that affection toward me. I had such conflicted emotions. I loved Carol and wanted to make her happy, but knew in my heart that I could not give her what she needed. Like a coward, I let the relationship continue to grow.

One night, after a date, we were back in our dorms talking on the hall pay phones. She kidded me by saying something like, surely you're not a virgin? I hesitated too long in my reply, which Carol took to mean, yes. It was true. I had not been with a woman but also knew there was no way that I could share with her how sexually active I had been in the past with men — multiple, nameless men. I felt so much shame. I knew as much as I loved Carol that I would only hurt her. And eventually, I did. And yet our friendship survived. In time, the embarrassing situation I had placed her in and the hurt that I had caused her took a back seat to the love she still felt for me. We were in our last year of college and she handled the breakup with grace. She squelched the rumors about me and became my protector. To this day, we are still friends, and my love for her has not wavered.

Her roommate Billye, also in the music department, was more of a risk taker, and she had her share of secrets, too. This bonded the three of us, and we have remained close for more than 40 years. In 1970, Billye, Carol and I came to Belmont University as freshmen, and although all three of us were in the music department, Billye was definitely (and still is) one of their shining stars. In the early 1980s, Billye and her family moved to Chattanooga and built a home on Signal Mountain. I had been working in the design field for some time and came to assist — something I have done through all of her moves. Then in November 1989, I was fortunate to hear her perform Poulenc's *Gloria* with the Chattanooga Symphony at the Tivoli. It was such a thrill to see her name displayed on the marquee. Her husband had already been transferred to Mobile and shortly after the concert, she joined him.

Billye, Carol and Ron

Carol, Billye and I have traveled together many times over the years — and with our birthdays just a few weeks apart, we celebrated turning 50 together with a weeklong cruise. Through the good times and the bad, we have remained strong knowing we are always there for each other. However, as close as we are, and even through years of confessions, I have never shared my entire past with them. In my heart, I know they will continue to love me in spite of my sins. And yet, as I continue to think back on the life that I have led, I often wonder if I even love myself.

Here I sit, singing my song,
Wondering if anyone, will ever sing along.
Here I sit, playing my tune,
Wishing and waiting, on the bright moon.

I entered Belmont as a music major in piano and voice. My high school piano teacher, a fellow First Baptist Church member, did her best to prepare me for the piano audition, as did my high school music teacher for the vocal audition. I began as a piano major in 1970 with a grandmotherly-type professor that wielded a ruler — she often used to swat my knuckles. The following year, I changed professors to a very intense gentleman, whose wife felt obligated to give me a reality check when she made a beeline for me at an event. The conversation began by asking me to confirm my father owned an insurance agency. She then delivered the one-two punch by asking if I had ever considered going into the family business — followed by her thought that I might be more suited for insurance than music.

Eventually, I did change my major, from piano to voice. This resulted in being called into the Dean's office. He said that I had talent — but felt I needed to change professors to improve. My new professor was also a member of my home church. His one frustration with me was not that I sang in the bass/baritone range, but that my speaking voice sounded like a tenor. It became quite comical when he insisted I speak in a deeper register when addressing him.

I was offered the chance to sing with the newly formed Belmont Chorale, a touring choir directed by the head of the music department. We would perform in various churches locally as well as out of state. Our more serious program would be performed in the church's sanctuary, followed by a lighter program in the fellowship hall of the church. That program allowed for solo and duets of more secular music. I would often be featured and sometimes would sing one of my original compositions. But there were also times that my songs would be sung by two of our female chorale members.

One of the more humorous numbers was a duet between myself and a female choir member. We chose the song, *Sisters,* from the movie *White Christmas.* I would slip on a dress and wig. My duet partner, not one to be considered petite, and I could pass as sisters. With an umbrella in hand, opened and turned to hide our faces, we would enter singing. The audience would break out into laughter once we raised our umbrellas and let them in on the joke. Members of the church's congregation would put

Ron with mother Joyce, Grandmother and Aunt Bobbye

us up for the night in their homes, and I can still remember two young boys talking about who was coming home with them after a concert. One boy pointed to his lodgers while the other, pointing to me, said: "We've got one of the sisters!"

When my parents had the opportunity to see me perform that number locally, my mother commented on how much I resembled her baby sister, Bobbye. Looking at her photos, I had to agree. The parents of my girlfriend, Carol, were also in attendance. Her father's comment to his wife pretty well summed it up. He said: "We need to keep an eye on him." The only negative thing I ever heard regarding my first drag performance was from a fellow chorale member, a rather prissy upperclassman, that thought it was embarrassing and distasteful. I wonder if he thought the same of Bing Crosby and Danny Kaye, who pantomimed the duet in the movie. Fortunately, our director disagreed, and we continued to perform that number several times during the season.

♬

My home church, First Baptist, had a small mission located not too far from the main church campus. Carroll Street Chapel met in a historic church building that had been built when grand homes were its neighbors. However, an interstate came through and divided the neighborhood. The homes were torn down and replaced by low-income housing, which created a congregation of elderly whites and younger African-Americans.

As a music student in my sophomore year, I was offered the part-time position as Carroll Street Chapel's music director by my Western Civilization professor. He served as the minister and his wife, the Dean of Women at Belmont, taught Sunday School. There was also a serious-minded Belmont student who briefly served as the associate pastor. This young man and I lived in the same dorm, and nightly he would step into the hall utility closet to pray. One evening, some pranksters open the door of the closet, tossed in a lit firecracker and closed the door. The poor young man felt he had witnessed the second coming as he frantically fled from what had become his sanctuary into the hallway of onlookers.

I will admit to not being the best of students. I did fine in classes that interested me but barely got by and sometimes failed in those that did not. Western Civilization was the first of my failures, although the second time around with a different professor, I passed with flying colors. One Sunday morning, the parents of my pastor/professor visited Carroll Street Chapel. His wife introduced me to them with the explanation that I had been one of his students, adding the tagline: "But he failed his class." I remained at Carroll Street Chapel longer than my professor and was delighted to have the opportunity to welcome his replacement.

The new pastor arrived with his family, and the church seemed to take on a friendlier atmosphere. He was kind and gracious, and his wife was delightful. I immediately clicked with them and became more comfortable in my position.

I claimed a small room behind the pulpit for my office. It had been a changing room for baptisms, complete with an old wall-hung porcelain sink. I painted the room bright red, with white trim. There was a beat-up table that I also painted and used for my desk. This made the rest of the building feel even more rundown — a thought I expressed to my father, who wanted to see for himself. The result led him to meet with the pastor of our mother church and insist that he also take a look. He expressed to him that we, as a church, should be embarrassed to have our name attached to something that we let fall into such disrepair. It did not take long before they had rounded up the church deacons to come, make repairs, and put on a fresh coat of paint where it was needed. For me, the church felt like it was coming back to life.

One Sunday morning, as the prelude played and the choir took their seats, the pastor stepped into my office and startled me by leaning in to give me a hug. He then tried to kiss me, as his hands began exploring. I pulled away, said it was time to begin the service, and walked out. Through the entire service, my mind replayed what had just happened. As I looked out into the congregation and saw his family, I knew I had to decide on the best way to handle this situation. Part of me wanted to step up to the podium and expose his behavior, but I knew that wasn't possible. It would ruin him, along with his marriage. Plus, I had no idea what it would mean for the church.

I came to the conclusion that the best thing I could do would be to simply talk with him about this and explain that it could not happen again. At 21 years old, I was no longer a minor. I did not have to put up with unwanted advances. It was not that I felt violated or traumatized, having been down this road before. Still, this was different. I cared for his family and did not want to hurt them. He had acted recklessly, and that almost always guarantees getting caught. It had to stop.

My father never gave me a reason, but I knew he was not fond of my pastor. I wonder if he saw though his facade. He did not warn me or forbid me to have anything to do with him, as he had done with Kenny, a childhood friend of mine. Clearly my father had thought years earlier that my childhood friend was "different" and that if he kept us apart, I might not become like him. It was probably the same protective radar that made him leery of the mission pastor. Or maybe he recognized something in him that he saw in himself.

It was the following week before I could speak with the minister alone. I had prepared what I wanted to say but felt that he did not want to listen. Since I was still a college student and needed the part-time job's income, I was not ready to leave Carroll Street. Plus, I enjoyed working there and did not want to lose my job. Sex had always been a part of my church experience, starting with the first man who molested me when I was 7 years old. Would one more man having his way with me at church make that much of a difference? I decided I needed to change my way of thinking and simply look at this as just part of my job description. Church = Sex. However, in my heart, I knew it could not continue. Eventually I would need to leave.

♫

I lived in the dormitory at Belmont for my first two years but had to move home for my junior year. My father had taken a leap of faith and had left his job to start a new business. My parents thought everything would be fine ... until the firm my mother worked for closed. I can only imagine the fears and struggles they had. And yet I was not the least bit happy about moving back home.

Along with the part-time music director's job at Carroll Street Chapel, I found a part-time retail position at Strobel's Music Shop in the Arcade. The year was 1973, and the store was located in my old stomping ground of downtown Nashville.

Going into Strobel's was like stepping back in time. The store's main level was painted a dark gray-green color. Because a second floor had been created, it had a rather low ceiling. Filing cabinets of sheet music and music books were still full from the days when it was the go-to place for musicians. The second floor, also with a low ceiling, had desks and practice rooms that were no longer used. The desks still had papers and files on top, as if the workers had left for lunch one day and never returned, giving the place an eerie, apocalyptic feeling. The third floor, also unused, had been the repair shop and opened directly off the Arcade's upper balcony. Again, it appeared as if, one day, workers had been busy at their jobs and then simply disappeared.

My boss was one of the Strobel sons. According to him, he had been a dancer on Broadway and clearly resented being called home to run the family business. His heart, mind and patience were not into retail, and in a very short time he stopped coming in and let me handle things. The customers were an eclectic mix that included little old lady piano teachers, along with strippers who worked in the bars of Printer's Alley one block away.

There was one young man who came by often to play the guitars. He wanted desperately to buy a guitar but was unable to come up with the money. One day he surprised me with an offer to work off the debt. I told him that I was not hiring and the dying business did not need another employee. I'll admit that I was surprised when he then offered to trade guitar payments for sex, and even more surprised when I heard myself agreeing to his proposition. So I bought the guitar, and he made weekly installments to me on the deserted second floor, with a sign on the locked door saying, *Be Back in a Minute*.

Between the two jobs, I was able to afford the shared rent during my senior year for an apartment across from Belmont's campus with my fellow

Roommates John and Ron

music student and friend, John. The two-bedroom, one bath, second floor apartment at Colonial Village may have been a dump, but it was ours. The front door could be closed and locked and yet, if bumped with your backside, it would still open. The hot water heater was exposed in the kitchen and generated enough heat for the whole apartment in the winter months. Of course, it competed with the window air conditioner during the summer months. A double bed with a missing leg had been left in the apartment and became mine. Other furnishings came from my parents' attic or were "borrowed" from a closed-off and rumored to be condemned dormitory at Belmont.

So many memories are connected to this apartment. I was living there when my roommate, John, and our friend, Larry, took me to my first gay bar, The Other Side. I remember sitting in a booth with a syrupy Singapore Sling in the glass before me. I was nervous and excited at the realization there were other men who looked like me, that had the same feelings as me, and could be themselves somewhere other than in a public restroom. It was also when I finally admitted to myself and my friends that I was gay.

It was in that apartment that I learned the meaning of the term, "commode-hugging drunk," as we started drinking Screwdrivers one night and ran out of vodka. Someone had the brilliant idea to continue making them, substituting gin for vodka. The combination had me praying to the porcelain god for mercy. This was also the apartment where I woke one morning to find that Kenny, my friend from elementary school, had come home with my roommate, John. Kenny was the friend that my father told me to stay away from as a child. I now realize that my father saw in Kenny the same "sissy" traits that he saw in his own son — and now, nearly 10 years later, Kenny and I discovered just how much alike we had been all along. John and Kenny's relationship did not last long, and soon John had moved on to an Asian transgendered entertainer. His taste had always been eclectic, and he was able to move fluidly between women and men.

Carol, Ron, Nita Payne and Joyce

This was also the apartment where one night I confessed to Carol and told her a version of my truth. Her reaction ran the gamut of emotions, but after several weeks we were able to regain our friendship. Many of our fellow students would pop in and hang out in our apartment. John's friend Larry became a regular, and now that I had confessed to Carol, I felt more comfortable around Larry and found we had more in common than John and I. Of course, one thing we had in common was John. I think there were times that John enjoyed being the object of occasional desire from both of us.

The chorale, in 1973, went on a three-week European tour that began in St. Moritz, Switzerland, for a weeklong festival with other choirs, followed by a tour and performances in Austria and Italy. I bring this up simply because of an event that took place between me and my *Sisters* big-boned duet partner, who instigated a scandal.

We had an attractive, personable British tour director on this journey. My duet partner had already expressed an attraction to him, and she was not alone. I felt the same way, and one night went to his room alone. We sat and

Larry and John

talked for quite some time, and I made a verbal pass at him, to which he responded positively but also said because of his job, nothing could happen. I was disappointed but understood and respected his position. Neither of us were aware that my duet partner had been eavesdropping at the door. What and how much she heard, I'll never know, but I was seated closest to the door so assumed that she at least heard my side of the conversation. Whatever she heard was enough to get the rumors started. The gossip gained momentum and eventually, most everyone knew some version of that conversation. The tour director and I both denied the accusations, and I retaliated by saying awful things about my fellow chorale partner.

When all of that came about, I had two roommates on that leg of the tour. One was my housemate, John, who could not have cared less about the gossip even though he knew it to be true. The other was the boy that would knock on my door at night and then swear it would never happen again. He chose to distance himself from me and asked to switch rooms, for fear someone might realize what he had been trying so hard to hide.

John, Larry and I decided to move in together and found a larger apartment in south Nashville. Over the next decade, the three of us acted as if there was a revolving door to our home and would find ourselves living solo, in pairs and at times, as a trio. This new apartment was spacious, with three bedrooms. My parents purchased "real" bedroom furniture for me and eventually, we all upgraded from the original secondhand pieces that graced our first home.

Our chameleon roommate, John, decided he wanted to perform in drag at a new gay bar. The Delta Queen was in a barn-like building that faced Broadway and sat next door to my church. He chose the stage name Lady Vanessa and, honestly, John never looked more butch than when he put on the wig and gown. Sometimes handsome men do not make pretty women, and this was the case. Plus, he walked as if he had a corncob inserted into his anus. His one and only performance was comical, although that had not been his intention. I will admit being relentless in my making fun of him — so much so that he dared me to do better, and I accepted his challenge.

I had made friends with Doug, the doorman at The Other Side, my first gay bar experience. When I told him of my intention to perform at a drag amateur show, he offered to help. We shopped for fabric and patterns, and he made my two dresses. One was an orange print caftan and the other, a peach satin gown. Doug helped me find a wig, and he and friends of his helped with my makeup.

Each contestant on amateur night could perform two numbers, on which they were judged. The night's winner was invited to be a guest performer in the weekend show. I chose songs from my two favorite albums, Carole King's *Tapestry* and Bette Midler's self-titled second album. Bette's version of the classic *Skylark* was my slow number in my elegant peach satin gown. But it was Carole King's *I Feel The Earth Move* that brought down the house. I'll admit to being a bit nervous, and maybe my dancing seemed a tad frantic. Regardless, it was good enough to be that night's winner and to be asked to perform with the regular cast in the upcoming weekend's show.

Many of the drag queens of that era chose stage names that could be male or female, such as Kerry Dennis, Charlie Brown, Lenny Latoke, Danny Ross. I followed suit and chose Lyn Michaels as my stage name. Needless to say, my success caused a bit of a rift between John and me, but in time he moved on to other things and became supportive. I enjoyed performing, but then one night a mysterious fire happened, and The Delta Queen burned to the ground. The vacant property then became an overflow parking lot for my church.

Lyn Michaels

I was most comfortable in a gay bar environment if I was performing or helping Doug take money at the door. I even helped serve food when the bar hosted a New Year's breakfast after the clock struck midnight. But, as myself, I felt very insecure and found myself expressing my feelings in the only way I knew how, through the lyrics of my songs.

TALK TO ME

What am I doing here? I know the evening will end the same.
What am I doing here? Is lonely the word or do I still believe, I'll meet
Mr. Right?
Talk to me, won't somebody, talk to me?
Don't judge me until you've heard my story, talk to me.
Tell me those lies that no one believe but everyone wants to hear.
Talk to me, talk to me.

What do I hope to find, searching in a bar of strangers?
Do I still expect a white knight, to sweep me off my feet?
Talk to me, won't somebody talk to me?
Tell me that you need me tonight, let me see it in your eyes.
I'll play the game, one more time,
Don't ignore me, don't ignore me tonight.

There's a panicked look on my face, desperation in my voice.
I know I'll hate myself in the morning, but tonight, won't someone
take a chance with me?

Don't judge me until you've heard my story, talk to me.
Tell me those lies that no one believes but everyone wants to hear.
Talk to me, talk to me.

What am I doing here? I know the evening will end the same.
What am I doing here? Is lonely the word or do I still believe I'll meet,
Mr. Right?

John was the first to move out. Larry and I, unable to make up the difference in rent, moved a few doors down into a smaller, two-bedroom unit. It was in this apartment that my parents wanted to surprise me with a graduation gift of a piano. They worked with Larry to coordinate that surprise. I should have graduated the previous spring but decided, in my senior year, to change my major. At that time the only options for a music major were performance, church or teaching, and none of those seemed appealing anymore. I switched to business, which meant I needed to go one more semester to pick up the requisite courses to be able to graduate. Belmont did not offer a winter graduation at that time, so I had to wait until the spring of 1975 to walk down the aisle and pick up my diploma.

SIX

POST COLLEGE

AGE 23+

Larry had begun working the front desk at a nearby Holiday Inn and had become friends with the dining room manager. His mistake came when he introduced me to "Jay," who had recently been involved with someone who had ended their relationship. I was probably just a rebound for him but, as was my pattern back then, when shown a little attention I was all in and didn't think twice.

"Jay" lived in his parents' home on the opposite side of town. They had taken their bedroom furniture and very little else and moved to Texas. Their plan was to return one day, so they wanted "Jay" to live in and maintain the family home until their return. When he asked me to move in with him, I jumped at the chance. His parents' bedroom was the only room without furniture, which meant my bedroom suite as well as my piano ended up in that small room.

"Jay" worked late most nights, but I was more than happy to be waiting up for him when he got home. And yes, we had conflicting work hours. And the home, far off my beaten path, often gave me a feeling of isolation. I was still determined to make this relationship succeed. However, it did not take long before there were cracks in my happy little world.

One thing he neglected to tell me was that his younger sister, who was away at college in a neighboring town, came home most weekends. He also forgot to mention that his older sister, living in a family home in an adjoining state, also came home on a regular basis. Plus, there was his mother, not happy in Texas, who would come home for a couple of weeks at a time. And when any of his family was back in Nashville, his cousin and her young son would be over at the house, morning, noon and night.

Unfortunately, "Jay" was very closeted, so when his family was in town, I had to sleep in that upstairs bedroom where all of my furnishings were stored. Since "Jay" worked late most nights, I was left at home with his two sisters, mother, cousin, and her young son. I actually saw more of them than I did of "Jay." The more I complained to him, the more I would hear about his ex and realize he was not over him, even though he had hurt him badly. He was still in love with him, and it made me feel as if I would never fully take his place.

When our relationship felt it was being held together by Band-Aids, I decided I had to move out. I think "Jay" was relieved because it had been so stressful for him, trying to keep me happy while living a lie in front of his family. I went back to the apartment complex I had left just a few months earlier and rented a one-bedroom unit across the parking lot from my former roommate, Larry.

During the brief time "Jay" and I lived together, I purchased several pieces of furniture for us. They were things he had loved, and I wanted to make him happy. I bought things for what was supposed to be our home. And when we broke up, amicably, we divided the purchases. I took the few that would fit in my new small apartment, with the agreement that I could pick up the remainder when I had the space.

Another pattern of mine in relationships: I try to buy love. It really is not my intention, but it always seems to come down to that. I give gifts because I want to, and at the beginning the gift receiver is thrilled. Then it reaches the point of them expecting the gifts, followed by asking for more. I begin to feel taken advantage of and back down my spending. They in turn become angry at being cut off.

As with many relationships, the breakup eventually becomes bitter, especially when it seems the other party has moved on. That is what happened with us. Even though "Jay" would sometimes spend the night with me, I realized he was moving on with his life. I decided I should go ahead and get the rest of my things out of his family's home, as our relationship was disintegrating quickly. He had begun avoiding me and had started acting as if the pieces I had left in his home were now his. I finally broke down and explained this to my mother. I knew his work schedule and the fact that his mother was in town. I asked my mother to call her to see if the two of us could meet and try to work things out.

At first his mother was gracious. But his two sisters, eavesdropping from the other room, kept making loud comments. "Jay" had given his family the impression he had purchased those items and that he had let me live there rent free. He also had told them I had become so attached to him that I had made him uncomfortable, wanting more than the friendship he was willing to offer.

His mother began to quote Scripture condemning my actions, but my mother could match her word for word, even finishing the Scripture verses. My mother also said that the relationship between their sons was not what we were there to discuss. She reminded his mother we had come only for the furniture pieces that were mine.

His family had believed his lies regarding the purchases, but when we showed his mother my canceled checks as well as canceled rent checks made out to "Jay," there was not much else she could say. We loaded up the few pieces while his sisters continued to belittle me and called me a fag — saying their brother was only trying to help me and that he wasn't queer. They also had "Jay" on the phone, and he was yelling and furious I had chosen to do this while he was at work.

Finally, my mother had enough. She said, regardless of what they think, that she loves me and will stand by me and that they should feel the same about their son and brother. She ended the conversation by saying, if there was nothing between their sons, they should ask "Jay" why he spent the previous night with me. His family knew he had not come home the night before, and whether they would admit it or not, they had finally realized that possibly not every word coming out of my mouth was a lie.

I felt such relief on the way home. It was like a huge weight had been lifted off me. I had finally admitted to my mother what she already knew. And I had no other connection to "Jay" and felt I could finally move on with my life. When we got home, I could tell my father was visibly upset. It seems "Jay" had chosen to retaliate and had called my dad. I'm not sure of everything he said, but he did confirm that I was homosexual. I think back now on all of the times we had been down this road, even though I never admitted to being gay. It should not have been a surprise, and yet having his suspicions confirmed brought my dad to tears. I did not know what to say or how to fix this.

I'm gathering old newspapers, to pack the dishes in,
Stopped by the liquor store, for empty boxes, and a fifth of gin.
Grabbed up a few of my things and said, "I'm giving up on men."
It's moving day, and I'm moving out again.

♫

John, the college roommate, aka "the Chameleon," was back in my and Larry's lives, and the three of us decided to move in together again. There was a new apartment complex being built nearby, where we rented a three-bedroom, two-bath flat. It had stylish Harvest Gold appliances and carpeting popular during the 1970s, and we had upgraded our furnishings once again to complement our brand-new space.

Larry and Ron

Ron and John

My parents built an addition to their home. I drew the plans for the new master bedroom with two large walk-in closets. I left the existing master bath, where just a few years earlier I had showered with the young sailor whom I had picked up in the park, and divided the original master bedroom into a new bath for my mother and a large utility room. New carpet, paint and a few added furnishings updated the house. A friend, after seeing the improvements, mentioned a local design school to me.

I enrolled at O'More School of Design the summer after my spring graduation from Belmont.

I had left the familiarity of Carroll Street Chapel in 1975 for the unknown of Southgate Baptist Church. It was a fairly new church congregation that met in an old home, located in South Nashville. They had added a large, concrete-block multipurpose room on the back that served as the sanctuary.

I learned many of the members came from other area churches. It did not take long to realize most had become unhappy with their previous churches and came together to be unhappy under one roof. As with any church congregation, there were some wonderful people as well as those that seemed impossible to please.

I was blessed to feel an immediate connection with the church pianist and her husband. Her sister and parents were also supportive. The church organist and several of the choir members took me under their wing and were very caring.

I never quite felt connected to the pastor but still thought we had a good working relationship. It was not long before I began to hear the snide remarks regarding his lack of fashion sense, and how he favored matching his socks with his dress shirts. Baby blue or yellow would often be peeking out from below the cuffs of his pants. I don't remember the gift the church gave me that Christmas, but I clearly remember they purchased a suit, shirt, tie and even dark socks for the pastor. Shortly thereafter, the church took a vote to let him go.

There were also grumblings about me from day one. It seemed one of the families in the church had a relative that they thought should have had my job. They had voiced their opinion on several occasions. They even accosted me after a service and blamed me for choosing the wrong invitational hymn that day. A friend of theirs was visiting that morning, and they were sure he had felt the Lord's call. However, they say he changed his mind because of my poorly chosen closing hymn.

The matriarch of the grumblers decided to pepper me with awkward questions and began by asking if I was married. I said no. "So, you graduated high school and didn't get married?" "No, ma'am." She continued with: "You graduated college and still didn't marry?" Again, I replied: "No, ma'am." She then looked me straight in the eye, with a knowing smile, as she asked her final question: "And now (pause) you're going to Interior Design School?" With a grunt, she turned and walked away before I could answer.

Guest preachers began appearing weekly trying to win favor. The one that was my downfall was a country "hellfire and damnation" type. He began the service by asking everyone to hold up their Bibles in the air. I, along with several of my choir members, had left my Bible in the choir room. He glanced back at me, then said: "If you forgot your Bible, then hold up your hymnal." Of course, I had my hymnal, but felt very awkward on the platform behind him and hesitated to raise it over my head. He then robustly said: "Now, shake it. Shake it in the face of the devil." This type of preaching was so foreign to me that not only did I feel out of place, I felt like a spotlight was shining on me. After the service, I walked to my car and found I had two flat tires, on opposite sides. I might not have questioned one flat tire, but two had me wondering if it was the devil's handiwork or one of the church members.

A few weeks later, I was informed that a vote was to take place to decide if I should also be let go. As miserable as the experience had been, I was not ready to be fired. That Sunday morning, when I led the choir into the sanctuary, I was blown away by the attendance. There was not an empty seat in the room. The grumblers had been calling in favors and rounded up everyone they could think of to cast a vote. My dear parents came out to support me and sat close to the front. The outcome of the vote resulted in that being my last service at Southgate. The pianist and organist showed their support for me by resigning. I was told there were a few others that felt it was time, once again, to change churches.

In spite of everything bad that had happened in my past that was connected to a church, I still wanted and needed a church home.

Before you criticize others, saying things that are not true,
Why don't you look in the mirror and search yourself through and through.
Please don't judge another person, your opinion may be wrong,
And your thoughtless, cruel words, may become your judgement song.

As my first year at O'More came to a close, I applied to Parsons School of Design in New York and found myself accepted. I began to research and decided that I could live at the YMCA until finding an apartment and roommate to share expenses. I had picked up a paperback book titled *New York On 5 Dollars A Day* (remember, this was 1976), and although a bit scared, I was excited about the possibility of moving away. Needless to say, my father was not thrilled and tried his best to talk me out of it. I had been a student at Belmont for five years and then O'More for one year. So when my father purchased a second insurance agency and expressed his need for me to help run it and told me what my salary would be, I finally relented and said goodbye to design and hello to the world of insurance.

With a decent paycheck, I had the opportunity to purchase a brand-new condominium west of town, just a few miles farther out than my family home. It was a brand-new two-bedroom townhome with garage. I picked out many of the finishing touches and was proud of the final result. The downside was the location. While it later became a booming area, it was anything but that when I moved in. Not only was shopping limited, but my friends all complained about having to drive out so far to visit.

I left Larry and John behind. John was in a relationship that eventually led to his first marriage. He asked me to be a groomsman, and I agreed before realizing he expected us to wear yellow tuxedos. Larry remembers me saying that I did not want him to move with me. Sadly, I can't remember either way. But I did move in by myself, and Larry eventually moved back to his hometown in Florida.

I wasn't alone for long. I met Bob, a young man who worked in the men's department at Cain-Sloan department store downtown. Bob and I had a few dates, and he lived in an efficiency apartment in the Vanderbilt area, across the street from where I would move a year later and eventually open two businesses.

Bob showed me attention. I was hooked and insisted he move in with me. He gave up his apartment, but in just a few months, I knew I could not live with him. I was miserable and did not even want to come home knowing he was there. I finally told him so, and having the upper hand, asked him

Groomsman Ron in yellow tux

to move. I felt terrible, because I had convinced him to give up his home, moved him in with me, and now I was telling him he had to move out.

ONE-SIDED LOVE AFFAIR

Well, it's a one-sided, I do for you, you don't do for me, kind of love affair.
Where you keep what you've got, all to yourself,
and anything that's mine, you expect me to share.

Yes, it's another one of those, how did I get myself into this,
And more importantly, how do I get myself out, nightmare.
And the scary part of it is, that I think I'm in love, but I also think,
You just don't care.

What starts out as generosity, or a helping hand,
Turns into a, take it for granted, or how about a little more.
And what starts out as a hot sultry night, a hot-blooded lover,
Ends up strictly platonic, and becomes such a bore.

Still I keep hanging on, maybe just in hopes, you'll finally realize,
that I love you more,
than any other natural born fool, you'll ever find,
And let me tell you, in case you didn't know, it's a chore.

Well, I wish I could say, this is positively the very last time,
I'll let myself get into this messy situation.
And that I'll never let my eyes wander,
or my heart wait in such anticipation.
I'll no longer settle for anything less than love in return,
no more just infatuation.
Because my body can't take the symptoms of love, or hate, or hate,
or love, no contradictions.

I have to keep asking myself, what is it about me,
that always seem to attract,
that special kind of louse?
And why do I find the necessity to always invite them
to move into my house?

♫

I stayed in that condo for a little over a year and worked for my dad's insurance agency full-time after losing my church job. And if that wasn't enough, I performed in drag at The Other Side. I had now become a cast member, which required late-afternoon rehearsals. I would arrive in a suit straight from the office, and my fellow castmates looked as if they had just rolled out of bed, which most had. I became the emcee for the Wednesday night amateur show. This was how I got my start a few years earlier at The Delta Queen. You can imagine my surprise when I found, after my father passed away, in the box of family photos, pictures of my teenage dad in a dress. I guess that's just one more thing we never knew we had in common.

I loved to find the most dramatic numbers to perform, often piecing two songs together. This was back in the day where the music was on reel-to-reel tapes, and I had a friend who would record my selections for me. I remember he loved a challenge, but when I told him I wanted to piece together Carly Simon's *You're So Vain* with Linda Ronstadt's *You're No Good*, he thought I had lost my mind. Two songs by two different vocalists — there was no way that it could work. And yet it did, and became one of my most popular numbers.

Another fun and very energetic number connected with my Southern Baptist roots. I had the good fortune to see the musical, *Bubbling Brown Sugar* on Broadway and purchased the soundtrack. One of my favorite hymns, *His Eye Is On The Sparrow*, has a somber beginning but builds to

Young Bob with his cousin, Maude

a very rousing version in the production. So with a burgundy choir robe borrowed from Carroll Street Chapel, along with a handheld funeral home fan, I performed the hell out of that gospel hymn. The first time I pantomimed that number, the stage at the Other Side had an addition of a runway leading into the dance floor. As the number continued to build, and I became filled with the Holy Spirit, I ran from the back of the stage, down that runway, and jumped onto the dance floor to the screams and applause of the audience. The fact that I broke the heel of my shoe in the process did not matter. I had given the crowd something to talk about for quite some time.

The runway had been built for the annual Miss Gay Nashville pageant. The following year, the club owner encouraged me to enter the competition. A friend of mine had won the previous year, and the contest had been covered by our local paper. The article had not only used my friend's stage name but his birth name as well. They had also gone on to mention where he was employed. The following day, he was fired. Drag in the mid-1970s was not something most businesses wanted associated with their employees.

I did finally agree to enter the contest, but even though I did not dream of winning, I had made the club owner promise that I would **not** win. I could not have my name, especially my dad's insurance company, listed in an article. With those assurances in place, I got excited about competing. I had been letting my thick, dark hair grow longer, wanting to not have to deal with a wig, and had put together a tasteful wardrobe. The big-hair, over-the-top drag looks were taking a backseat to a more natural look. My look was more Suzanne Pleshette, during the *Bob Newhart Show* era.

I had opened a charge account at Grace's Shop for Ladies when I worked downtown at Strobel's Music Shop, often purchasing gifts for my mother there. Wanting special jewelry for the pageant, I found an Egyptian-style necklace and earrings that after the pageant became a lovely gift for my mom.

My reputation for unusual and dramatic musical numbers had me giving a great deal of thought about my talent selection — for which there was an individual award. I decided to try something that had not been done locally and began my number in full drag, pantomiming Shirley Bassey's version of *Nobody Does It Like Me* by Cy Coleman and Dorothy Fields from the 1973 musical *Seesaw.* The lyrics have an overall theme that has the singer confessing that regardless of the situation, they are going to make a mess of things.

As that song ended, an instrumental of *Send In The Clowns* from the Stephen Sondheim musical *A Little Night Music,* also from 1973, began to play. For that number, I sang in my own voice as I slipped out of my dress to reveal I was wearing a shirt and jeans underneath. I brushed out my hair, took off my eyelashes and makeup and, performing as myself, sang this heartbreaking ballad about misunderstanding. It seemed my years of misreading relationships had left me feeling a strong connection to this song.

After everyone had performed, the judges needed a bit of time to make their decision. The club owner came to me and told me that I had won, and asked what I wanted to do. I thanked him but again, told him that I could not win and to please choose someone else. When all of the contestants were brought back out to the stage, the emcee announced that I had won the talent portion. Another contestant had won for evening gown, then they announced the award for second runner-up. Next came the announcement for first runner-up, and my drag name was called. The judges' original choice for first runner-up was awarded the crown of Miss Gay Nashville — and true to form, his name and occupation were listed in the morning paper. But for First Runner-Up, only my stage name of Lyn Michaels made the news.

I will never forget my mother, after seeing the article in the paper, asked me why I did not win! I held on to that gold plastic trophy for a long time. Then one day, I threw it out, ready to forget my past.

The Other Side added a piano bar after the pageant, and the pianist would stop whatever song he was performing and start playing *Send in*

Lyn Michaels

the Clowns whenever I walked into the bar. That is still one of my favorite songs to this day.

One funny thing that happened during that period was the club needing to find a new insurance carrier, and they thought: Why not ask their very own drag queen insurance salesman? Somehow, I found the nerve to tell my dad about a club that I knew in need of insurance. We met with the club owner, who kept calling me "Lyn," but ultimately my dad was unable to help him.

Long after The Other Side had closed, I returned to the stage one final time when the current drag bar, The Cabaret, invited some of the "old-timers" to perform. I found myself overwhelmed by the amount of effort it took and decided to retire my tiara after that night.

I received a call from Carroll Street Chapel's newest pastor offering me the music director's position, which I gladly accepted. In the two years since my resignation from Carroll Street Chapel, the historic church building had been condemned and torn down. The dwindling congregation had moved across the interstate into a small rented building, which had originally been a residence. The one-story structure consisted of a central hall with two bedrooms on the left, used as classrooms. Drywall had been removed between the parlor and the dining room on the right, exposing the wiring and framework. This visually opened the combined rooms, creating a makeshift meeting room with rows of folding chairs and a center aisle. A kitchen in the back of the home also served as a classroom. Each of the rooms had a fireplace with a gas heater, which became my responsibility to light on cold winter mornings. I would turn on the gas, strike a long kitchen match, and pray I did not blow up the place.

There were only about 40 members remaining, and the choir's adult members were now gone. The remaining choir members consisted of eight African-American teenagers, some of whom had children of their own. We continued to sing traditional hymns during the service, but I let the teenagers teach me songs for their weekly anthems. It was definitely a challenge to learn those songs without the benefit of sheet music. Eventually, our pianist chose only to play the hymns for the service, leaving me to improvise as I tried to accompany the choir.

Having seen this in other churches, the choir wanted to begin the morning service with a processional down the center aisle as they sang. It could often be a bit comical as they tried to match each other's step, but we all would stifle our laughter because it meant so much to them.

I had an immediate bond with the preacher and felt it to be my most comfortable working relationship. We adapted to the needs of the

congregation instead of trying to make them conform to our past experiences of how things had always been done. His sermons connected with the uneducated and the intellectual. His wife remained at First Baptist during his tenure, leaving me to think of the two of us as the odd couple in Christian ministry.

The only conflict I had upon returning involved a Belmont student who was also a fellow First Baptist Church member. He volunteered his time at Carroll Street and had filled in as music director before I had been rehired. Although I did not know at the time, he resented me and thought the job should have been his.

My former college roommate, Larry, would often attend Carroll Street with me. We were the closest of friends but never romantically involved. I found myself in shock when the pastor pulled me aside to say there had been a complaint made by one of the members. He had been told that Larry and I had been seen hugging and kissing in one of the classrooms. I demanded to know who had started the rumor, since I knew it to be false. I learned the accusation had come from the Belmont student and immediately confronted him. He confessed that he had lied, hoping the scandal would have been enough for me to resign. He apologized, and although I was furious, I forgave him. I'm not sure he ever forgave himself, however.

Anyone who has been in the field of church work has probably seen or heard experiences similar to what I had encountered. My expectations were high, working with Christian people in a church environment. I had never imagined the drama that somehow always found me. Having been employed by one church or another for 10 years, I now found myself mentally, physically and spiritually exhausted. No longer did I think of this as my calling. I knew in my heart that the Lord had something else in mind for me. Finally, I left the small mission and returned to First Baptist. Eventually, a new building was built for Carroll Street — the name changed — and they gained their independence.

Ron and Larry

S E V E N

New Home — New Job — New Boyfriend

I don't think I could have been any more miserable than when working in my dad's insurance office. I was much more concerned about furniture placement in the office than about someone's auto or home insurance. I jumped at the chance in 1977 when he suggested one day that we walk a few blocks from our office to an auction taking place at the former Blood Bank building. At one time, the building had been a two-story, four-square home. Through the years, a one-story addition had been added that circled three sides of the first floor. And while the first floor was a maze of small rooms, many with sinks, the second floor had the original four-corner rooms with plastered-over fireplaces and 10-foot ceilings. I had no idea my father was considering buying the property. I am not sure he had thought it through himself.

The bidding began and very quickly stalled at a ridiculously low price. My dad startled me as he joined in the bidding. We almost fainted when the bidding closed and he had just purchased the property. My mind exploded with ideas, but one thing I knew for sure — I was going to move in!

He was still in shock when I announced I was selling my condo and moving into the second floor of the building. He could not understand why I would want to leave a brand-new place for this tired old building. The property was on a tiny lot with limited parking, but faced Broadway on one side and Division Street on the other. The Broadway entrance made the most sense for the insurance office, as it opened into the largest room in the entire building. This former waiting room was ideal for his two associates and me to have desks. There was a fireproof room at the back that became the file room. A couple of walls had to be removed to create a large-enough office for my dad, and we finished off two more small rooms with fresh paint and carpet. Finally, the office was complete, and we still had half of the first floor unused and in its original state.

Upstairs, one wall was removed that divided a corner room. This became my living room. Another corner room turned into my kitchen, with the remaining two rooms as bedrooms. There were two-half baths on that level, one of which had a hall leading to it where we added a shower stall and washer/dryer connections. I spent untold hours chipping plaster off two of the fireplaces, exposing the antique brick. The second floor made for an interesting apartment. With the unique history of the building's previous occupant, I wrote an article that was published in the *Christian Single* magazine titled, *I Live in the Blood Bank.*

I loved living in the Midtown area. In the late 1970s to mid 1980s, the area was not nearly as congested as it has now become. With the exception of a couple of restaurants and bars, most businesses were closed in the evening. My apartment was located just a couple of blocks from the Vanderbilt University campus, where I would walk to the student center to see films. I also joined a weight management class at Vandy and lost nearly 40 pounds. I would exercise daily and walk in the evenings to Hillsboro Village and back.

A woman contacted my dad regarding the vacant space on the Division Street side of the building. She had an idea for a bookstore and was curious to know if he had any interest in leasing a portion of the space. She stopped by and spoke with me about the theme of her store and presented it as focused on religion and Christian beliefs. I told her that my mother would be interested in that, which led her to invite both of us for lunch at her home.

The home was not large, but it sat on Jackson Boulevard, a prime Belle Meade street. We arrived and were led into the drawing room. When lunch was ready, we moved into the formal dining room where her maid, in full uniform, served cucumber sandwiches with the crust cut off, and tomato aspic. That was my first, and hopefully, last encounter with the gelatin salad.

Our hostess began to explain her thoughts on religion, which had very little to do with Christianity, and I could sense my mother doing her best to restrain her opinion. It was not the most productive of meetings, but still, my dad agreed to finish off the space and rent it to her. We had already given an unused office in the back half of the building to a friend who was a professor, writer and basically an artistic type. Our future tenant would turn up her nose and say "artist" as if she smelled manure. The relationship was already beginning to sour when she requested a separate bath be added so that she did not have to share with the "artist." My dad did go along with that, more for the sake of our friend than the arrogant soon-to-be tenant.

Her next request began her exit. The overly wide exterior door opened into the space instead of opening out, as codes would require in new construction. Because of the age of the building, the door was grandfathered in and did not have to be changed. She did not like that answer and went directly to codes. When she realized she was not going to win, she wrote my dad a letter and called him every unsavory name she could think of and accused him of having "illegal" business practices. My dad simply called her husband, who happened to be an attorney. He told him that someone had sent him a letter and after reading it, asked if he would have a good case for defamation of character. The attorney said most definitely and appeared chomping at the bit to go after the writer of this letter. My dad then told him that his wife had sent the letter. To which the husband asked: "How much would it take to get out of the lease?"

The Belle Meade matron opened her bookstore elsewhere, and we never had to deal with her, or her tomato aspic, again.

BELLE MEADE PROPER

Ever since I was a young boy, living on the other side of the tracks,
I always dreamed that one day, I'd leave West Meade and never look back.
I want to live in Belle Meade, don't you?

I want to be seen jogging up and down the boulevard,
By every BMW, Mercedes and Jaguar.
Oh, I want to live in Belle Meade Proper, don't you?

I want to be a member of the Belle Meade Country Club,
Be seen at the Swan Ball, and of course, Sperry's Pub.
I want to live in Belle Meade Proper, don't you?

Of course, I want a big house on the boulevard, too,
But if I can't, then I'll take Jackson, Lynnwood, even Leake Avenue,
As long as it's in Belle Meade Proper, it will do.

I wanna roll and roll and roll and roll, honey.
In all that old, old, old, old, old green money.
With my bank account in the black,
I'm gonna spend and spend and never look back.
'Cause, I'm gonna live in Belle Meade.

And if they won't let me move on in,
I'll marry a billion, zillion heiress and then,
I'll buy it all up, ain't it a pity?
I'll tear it all down, say goodbye Belle Meade City.
If I can't live in Belle Meade.
Give me that old thirty-seven-two-o-five,
I want to live in Belle Meade.

♫

The Division Street side of the building was now remodeled and vacant. My mother and I dreamed about starting a retail store in the space. We brought up that idea to my dad, who resisted over and over again. We finally wore him down, and the three of us began to discuss what type of store would be a good fit. The area was not in a shopping district, although there were a few good restaurants in the immediate vicinity and three blocks down was the Country Music Hall of Fame and "World Famous" Music Row.

Christmas had always been huge in our family. The abundance of riches on Christmas morning, along with every room in the house decorated, was a family tradition. We always visited any Christmas store when traveling, so it made perfect sense to us to open a year-round Christmas shop. Because of our location, it would appeal to the tourists. Also, being the only Christmas store in town, we felt people would drive into the Midtown area to shop.

My dad agreed, and even came up with the name, the Mistletoe Shop. He said he was only willing to put in $5,000 for inventory. We applied for our tax number and made plans to drive to Atlanta and shop at the gift market for stock. We met the most helpful woman in one of the showrooms, who assisted us with making a list of the necessary items to get started. When she ran the totals and it came to almost $5,000, my mother and I turned to my dad, who said: "Go ahead and place the orders." In June 1979, the

Mistletoe Shop opened and for the next 12 years was one of Nashville's favorite destinations.

For the first six months, I had to work part-time in my dad's insurance agency, and the rest of the time could be spent in the store. Eventually, he agreed to let me work full-time in the shop, which allowed my mom to work part-time. The shop started in two rooms and slowly began to take on more space. My dad eventually purchased a building one block away and moved his office so we could have the entire first floor. The basement served for storage, but during the busy season it would be opened to the customers. We may have started with a $5,000 investment, but by the fifth year our inventory ran closer to $200,000.

Working with my mother was wonderful. We were so in sync with our ideas and what we wanted and expected out of the shop. Of course, my mother had not worked full-time in several years and had filled her days with committees, organizations and, basically, a social life. This caused a bit of a problem when a couple of her friends began working part-time for us and would be invited to the same luncheon or event. But as the business grew, we were able to hire employees outside of her circle of friends.

I loved going to market, although it was difficult to resist shopping for more than Christmas merchandise. So many beautiful options were available at wholesale prices. The temptation was too great. Then there was the other temptation that involved many of the salesmen. I was in my prime 20s, and it was like a smorgasbord of available options. Many of the salesmen traveled during the year, and a few would spend the night with me when they were in town. It seemed that married men were the most eager.

There is one story that will give you an idea of my life during those times. Our store carried everything imaginable for Christmas. Ornaments, lights, trees, nutcrackers, china, cards and so much more. We also had a vast collection of nativities from all over the world. There was a company whose nativity set I wanted in our collection. They had requirements, as most companies do, that had to do with dollar amount of initial order. But in addition to that, they required the store to carry their other items, such as collectable figurines. Since we were a Christmas store, I was not interested in their other items, only the nativity and ornaments. The salesman apologized but still said no.

The head of the company was in the showroom that day and overheard my plea. He came over but also apologized for the policy. I asked: "As head of the company, can you not make an exception?" I felt serious eye contact happening and wondered where it would lead. He then said: "Let me think about it during the day, and come back by at closing and I'll have my answer." I thanked him and as I turned to go, he whispered: "Come alone."

That afternoon, as showrooms began to close, I told my mother I would be happy to run back by and see what he had decided. She was tired and anxious to get back to the motel, so I suggested that she rest, and that I'd be back in just a few minutes. He was waiting for me when I entered the showroom and said: "Follow me." We went down two floors to an area that had not been open for market, and I followed him into the men's room. He must have been anticipating my return all day, because it did not take long before he was finished and fastening his belt and straightening his tie. At that point, he said he would make the exception and true to his word, we opened an account and only had to purchase the nativity sets and ornaments. I remember having a strange feeling when the first of the nativity sets sold, and I thought back to what I went through to make that sale possible.

Our trips to market would always involve clothes shopping for my mother. I was raised shopping with her and could often convince her to be a little more daring in her choices. One of her favorite spots to shop in Atlanta was Loehmann's. Racks and racks of discounted women's clothing was a great draw. Since the dressing room was one large communal area, I was not allowed back there. I would be out front, scouring the racks and putting outfits together for her to try. It never failed that several of the women in the dressing room would take notice and ask who was helping her make selections. There would be times that some of the women would come out and ask if I would help them find a top that might work with a certain skirt. I would often spend hours as a "fashion consultant."

Back in Nashville, I was well-known by the management at one women's store for my skills, so much so that one day when a new employee tried to assist me, the manager came over and told her to leave me alone. She said: "He knows more than you do right now, so watch and learn."

Five years after opening the Mistletoe Shop, my mother developed cancer. I found out about it during one of those trips to market and our evening clothes shopping crawl. This particular trip, my mother kept going to each store's lingerie department. Finally, I asked what was this new obsession? She told me a lump had come up on her waist and the doctors thought that it was just a fatty tumor, but she would need to go into the hospital to have it removed. It turned out to be much more, as the doctors discovered she had renal cell cancer. One year later, she was gone. I kept the Mistletoe Shop for several more years, although it was never the same without her.

♫

Those years living above our Christmas store were often exciting, confusing, passionate, intense. I lived by myself for a while, then Larry lived with me for a bit. Several of the sales reps would spend the night with me when they were in town. Some slept in the guest room, and some found their way to my bed. At one point, even our UPS driver became a conquest. Or maybe it was the other way around, since he made the first move.

My ex, "Jay," reappeared in my life when he called for my help in getting a friend insurance after a DUI conviction. My dad's agency was able to help, and I was there when "Jay" and his friend "Dan" came in. It had been long enough for the sadness and anger of our breakup to be diminished. I remembered the friendship and enjoyed meeting "Dan" as well. That encounter led to dinner and then reconnecting and putting the past behind us.

"Dan" lived in a second-floor apartment above a residence on a street of beautiful and stately homes. He had a partner who was alcoholic, and the romance had long since faded. "Jay" was head over heels in love, but "Dan" not being 100 percent available left him frustrated. However, he was not one to give up. Eventually the obstacle moved out and "Jay" moved in. The apartment had been trashed over the past few years but, in time, it became a showplace.

I was over there often and helped any way I could with the decor. "Dan" was fun, and I don't believe he was ever totally faithful to "Jay." In fact, the first time he made a pass at me, I said no. I said no the second and third time,

Mardi Gras, New Orleans 1979

but finally relented by the fourth. But then I had made a pass at "Jay" and had succeeded, on several occasions. Our past relationship made things comfortable and familiar this time around. I was not purposely trying to come between them, and if I'm being totally honest, I did not want "Jay" back, and "Dan" was a slut and definitely not boyfriend material. I looked at it as just having fun.

In 1979 "Jay," "Dan," and another friend, Kerry, and I drove to New Orleans for Mardi Gras. Kerry was a good friend, and yet there were times I wondered why I considered him a friend. He said he had been overweight in his youth, but when we met he was very thin, often dressed in the tightest pants, and wore more makeup than most drag queens. He also drank heavily and had a caustic tongue that no one wanted directed at them. I remember one time, he was telling a story and pointed to me saying: "I can remember back when I was your size."

It was my first, and last, Mardi Gras. I could not believe the decadence. Nudity was rampant as we walked the crowded streets. Men and women would expose themselves for a necklace of plastic beads. Sex was taking place inside the bars, with crowds looking on. Pool tables were covered with plywood tops to protect them from the spilled beer and lubrication of the sexual partners. It was totally mind-blowing to me — I felt like I was in a 24-hour pornographic film.

As the four of us walked down the sidewalk, an attractive male with mustache, cowboy hat, jeans and boots walked by. He was staring at our foursome and then turned as he passed so that he could keep staring. "Dan" looked at me and said: "That guy is checking you out." With that, Kerry, never known to be the shy one, yelled to the cowboy and asked: "Which one of us are you interested in?" The cowboy pointed to me, and my friends motioned for him to join us. I panicked and said, under my breath "What do I do now?"

The cowboy's name was "Lou," and he was several years older than me. He had lived in New Orleans but was currently back home in Mississippi. And he clearly had been drinking, but that could be said about anyone at Mardi Gras. We stopped at the nearest bar, and it wasn't long before Kerry had made a conquest. "Jay" and "Dan" were doing their own thing, so "Lou" tried to whisper, over the speakers blaring Thelma Houston's, *Don't Leave Me This Way*, asking if I was ready to get out of there. I nodded yes and followed him out the door.

So many things were going through my head at the time. One, I loved that song. Two, with four of us sharing one motel room, it would be awkward to go back there. Three, because there were four us sharing that motel room, we only had two room keys and I wasn't one of the ones given a key. And four, I only had a few dollars and my driver's license in my pocket.

"Lou" had a place to go, and a car. He was staying with friends in an incredible home on the edge of the Garden District. I had no idea where we were, but I was so blown away by the home, it did not matter. The next morning, I felt differently. I woke before "Lou" and laid there wondering where I was, and tried to remember the name of the motel we had checked into the day before. This was before cellphones, so I had no way of contacting my friends. I thought of how similar this was to that church choir tour years earlier, when in New Orleans I followed a boy down one block and another, until I wasn't sure if I'd find my way back.

When "Lou" woke, we cleaned up and joined his friends for breakfast. I was so fascinated by their home. In fact, there was something about it that seemed vaguely familiar. What I learned was the house had been used in the Louis Malle film, *Pretty Baby*, released the previous year. The film had been notorious because of 12-year-old Brooke Shields playing a prostitute. I had seen the film just a few months earlier.

I spent the rest of my time on that New Orleans trip with "Lou." He acted as if he could not get enough of me — and as I now know, that was all I needed to make plans for our future. I was actually distraught when it came time to head home. I was so anxious to get home, just so that I could call him. We talked often, and he would come to Nashville to visit, or sometimes we met in Memphis.

I think back now wondering what was it about "Lou" that made me want him to be a part of my life. Was I attracted to him physically? I'll admit that at first I did find him appealing. Was it his personality? His intelligence? His fashion sense? God, no! Sadly, I realize the most appealing thing about him was the fact that he showed me attention. I was so desperate for a boyfriend, to be a couple like most of my friends, that I was willing to lower my standards (if I had any) and take the only man at that time who seemed to like me.

Merriam-Webster defines affection as *a feeling of liking and caring for someone or something: tender attachment.* They define attention as *an act of civility or courtesy, especially in courtship.* Each word begins with "a." Each has three syllables. Somehow, I have always thought of them as meaning the same. When someone showed me attention, or a courtesy, I immediately assumed it was affection or caring. I wonder if friends recognized that trait in me and warned others about being too nice to me, for fear it would have caused me to start picking out china patterns for my bridal registry.

With "Lou," I let myself believe that I actually had a boyfriend. Of course, he did drink quite a bit, and his grammar often made me cringe. But he was mine, all mine. Or so I thought.

LONG DISTANCE LOVER

You live so far away, it just doesn't seem fair.
Trapped by job and family, we're such a lonely pair.
If it wasn't for the telephone, to hear your voice each day,
I just don't think I'd make it, without hearing you say,
I love you.

Sometimes I get so lonely, wanting to be with you.
But you're just so far away, I don't know what to do.
With the telephone, in my hand, please answer, I pray,
That soon I can hold you, and kiss you, and say,
I love you.

Long distance lover, burning the telephone line.
Long distant lover, don't hang up, until you're mine.

We made plans for "Lou" to move to Nashville. Knowing he would need a job, he sent me a copy of his resume, which had a lapse of three years — something my dad picked up on immediately. We had an explanation, but it was lame. Bottom line: He had been in jail for a bit of embezzling. I convinced myself that no one's perfect, and with help from friends we found him a clerical job with the Methodist Board.

I now had a live-in boyfriend. One that rarely wanted to stay home. Most nights would either involve meeting friends for drinks at a bar or at their home. "Lou" could be a fun drunk at first, as his words would begin to slur. Then he would become very affectionate, but then move into a sloppy drunk, followed by him becoming belligerent, especially when anyone would suggest cutting off his supply. Was having a live-in boyfriend worth this?

At one Sunday afternoon party with friends, "Lou" disappeared for a bit. This was not unusual, and I got to the point of no longer trying to track him down for fear of causing a scene. These friends lived in an apartment building that had an attic. I learned, long after "Lou" and I parted, that he and another of the guests took a tour of the attic and were caught by others in a state of undress.

I knew "Lou" was cheating on me, but I was never able to catch him. Once we separated, I learned that several of my friends were aware of it but did not want to say anything for fear they would upset me. Not only had I moved "Lou" to Nashville and into my home, introducing him to my friends, but I also helped find him find a job. I even went so far as to move his mother from Tinsley, Mississippi to Nashville into a high-rise for seniors. She needed furniture and such, and I had helped with that, too. I kept thinking this was not the way I had imagined my life would be with a boyfriend.

I'm not blind to knowing that relationships can be hard. I don't even mind the give and take that often needs to occur — but I do object to feeling like I am usually the giver. I am so much more than just an ATM! A friend summed it up beautifully when she described the relationship, saying he "camped out" in my life. It's true. I think that I was so desperate to be in a relationship that I overlooked the overwhelming amount of baggage he brought to the table until the weight of it became unbearable.

I had finally reached my limit. I no longer wanted to fight, or hear another apology the morning after a drunken episode. I did not want anymore bruises, intentional or not — mentally or physically. I simply did not want to live like that any longer.

My mind was made up — he had to go. Once I convinced him that this was for the best, it became my job to find an apartment for him — and since he came without furniture, he would need to take some of my furniture with him. I kept telling myself it was worth it. I just needed him gone.

But he never really was gone. My friends had become his friends, and so there he would be at a party or dinner. Plus, there were times he would bang on my door or call me late into the night, drunk and begging for me to take him back. These actions made me dig my heels in even more at ending the relationship.

> *Well, I need some time alone,*
> *No, I don't want to be found.*
> *I need some time away from you,*
> *So don't ya be thinking 'bout coming around.*

After we separated, I met a young man who expressed an interest in me. After what I had been through, I was not ready for another relationship. And I definitely was not interested in him after he told me that previously he had been to my apartment: "With the guy that used to live there before, 'Lou' something or another." Since I was the one who had built out that apartment from when it had been offices for the Blood Bank, I told him that no one had lived there before me. This young man had done nothing wrong. "Lou" had lied to him, too, but I did not want anything or anyone that "Lou" had first. Finally, I had the overwhelming proof that he had never been faithful to me. I could not help but wonder how many guys he brought into my home when I was away on business.

I am not proud of my actions, but knowing "Lou" wanted me back, and knowing he had cheated on me numerous times, I became very spiteful. His new apartment was close by, and being just a one-bedroom it had only two windows, both facing the balcony walkway. Gathering my toothbrush and a change of clothes, I drove over to his complex and parked a few doors down. I looked through the sheer draperies of his living room and was delighted to see he was not alone. I waited in my car until the living room light went out and he and his guest had moved into the bedroom. Giving him a few moments, I gathered my things and knocked on his door. He came to the door partially dressed, startled to see me. I stood there, toothbrush in hand, and told him I had thought about what he had said and that if he still wanted me back, then I was ready. The look on his face was priceless. He stammered and said how happy he was, but still did not invite me in. That's when I asked if there was someone there. He knew he had been caught. Then, in a dramatic fashion, I said what a fool I had been and stormed off. Within minutes of getting home, he was at my door begging forgiveness. I sent him on his way. I knew clearly we would never be together again. In his mind, he thought he had missed the one opportunity to get me back. On top of that, he missed out on his evening's conquest. I have to say, sometimes revenge can be rather satisfying.

LOVE'S MORE THAN AN APOLOGY

We fuss and we fight, but before we say good night,
We always say, I love you.
We make each other mad, maybe it's not so bad,
We know, our love is true.
But still I wonder why, we make each other cry,
There must be a better way.
This hurtin' can't be love, I pray to heaven above,
Tomorrow, will be a better day.

No matter what we say, love shouldn't be this way.
No matter what we do, we apologize saying, I love you.
There ought to be some tenderness, and maybe, just a gentle kiss.
Harsh words, should never be.
Love's more, than an apology.

I continued to live above the Mistletoe Shop for a few more years. The parties in the early 1980s became fewer, and so did my dating. I spent a great deal of my time with "Jay" and "Dan." We ran around and found all sorts of trouble to get into, and then some nights we would just stay in and watch TV and talk. Occasionally another friend or two would join us, but more often than not, it was just the three of us.

My mother developed cancer during this time, and I needed the love and support of friends. Larry had gone to work for my dad in his new building one block down from the Christmas store. I began investing in rundown houses, in the up-and-coming area of East Nashville, where my friends "Jay" and "Dan" now lived. With each purchase, I would plan on moving but then would talk myself out of it. I would sell the houses long before renovations were completed.

My parents wanted to take me out for my 32nd birthday on December 11, 1984. My mother was getting weaker, and the cancer was taking its toll on all of us. I had recently purchased a wonderful small Spanish home with stucco exterior and a tile roof near Shelby Park. It reminded me of my Florida roots. The workmen were moving very slowly and asking for money in advance. I was so focused on my mother's health that I was not thinking clearly. I kept giving the contractor advances for work that was never going to happened.

As we sat in the restaurant waiting for our meal to arrive, my father tore into me about that project and my stupidity and everything I had done wrong in my life. My mother sat there in tears as I tried to defend myself. Finally, I reached my limit long before my birthday dinner arrived. I got up, kissed my mother, turned to my father and sarcastically said: "Thank you for a lovely time," and left. I drove home but parked my car a block away. I did not want him to find me. I wanted to hurt him, the way that

he had hurt my mother and me by his rant. But my phone did not ring, and there was never a knock on my door. The next day, my dad acted as if nothing had happened. I think that hurt even more.

I know my dad was at a loss with my mother's illness. He was used to fixing things, but this was something that could not be fixed. He was angry and let his anger lash out at me. I wanted to be understanding but

I, too, was at a loss about how to fix this. My mother was dying, and I could not imagine my world without her.

My dad and I never discussed our conflict. That was our modus operandi. I did apologize to my mother for leaving her that night. I knew it pained her to hear him belittle me over and over again. I'm sure she was thinking, how could she leave this world when my dad and I were unable to get along? But I assured her that his outburst was no big deal. I told her everything was fine. It had to be fine. I knew I had to make everything fine.

You always told me what I did wrong, didn't I do anything right?
If I said it was the middle of the day, you'd say, no, it's the middle of the night.
When I needed someone to understand, you'd always want to fight,
Don't tell me what I did wrong, didn't I do anything right?

♫

I attended an art opening in 1984 for portrait artist Goode P. Davis. His work was exquisite, and I immediately knew I wanted him to paint a portrait of my mother, who was undergoing cancer treatment. Even the price for one of his smaller paintings was out of my budget, but I did not let that stop me. I had enough for the 50 percent down payment and knew I could come up with the rest once it was completed.

I learned he had designed the magnificent stained-glass windows illuminating the sanctuary of First Baptist — my church home since age 4. The windows, colorful and abstract, are the polar opposite to his traditional portraits in oil.

Meeting with him at his home studio, I gave him photographs of my beautiful mother and asked that he paint her in the blue dress worn in one of the photos. I wanted a coral background and to have her wearing the diamond necklace my father had designed. The simple necklace consisted of three one-carat diamonds, symbolizing my mother, father and me. Mr. Davis, 79 years old and a bit ornery, assured me he had what he needed, so I left him to work his magic.

A few weeks later, he called to ask when my mother might sit for him. I reminded him that she was quite ill and that this would not be possible. He became angry with me and repeated that he needed her to come to his studio. I replied, saying once again that it could not, and would not, happen. He hung up on me.

Speaking with the people who had initially made the introduction, I was promised they would talk with him. The following week, he called asking me to stop by to see the progress and requested I bring her diamond necklace with me. Since I had not mentioned anything to my parents about the portrait, I found myself sneaking the jewelry out of the house and taking it to Mr. Davis. He insisted I leave the necklace with him for reference — which I did, after realizing I had no choice.

The portrait was near completion, and he had done a wonderful job capturing her likeness. However, he chose a green background instead of my suggestion of coral. When I commented that I did not have green in that room and wondered if it could be changed, he sternly said if I did not have green in the room, then I needed it. No, he would not make the change.

I did not have quite enough to pay off the balance when he called to say the portrait was complete, so I asked if I could go ahead and pick up her necklace, give him a partial payment, and the final payment within two weeks. He became very upset with me and said he would just go ahead and paint over the portrait if I did not come right away with the payment, adding that he wasn't even sure where he had put the necklace. Needless to say, I was on the verge of a total meltdown with my mother's health deteriorating, plus the thought of losing the portrait and his lack of concern for the missing three-carat diamond necklace. Devastated and emotional, I

told a family friend of the situation, who in turn loaned me enough money to pay off the balance. With a check in hand, I went to pick up the painting and was relieved to learn he had found the necklace. Even with the green background and the feeling that he had sent me to hell and back, I could not have been more pleased.

By the time the 1980s had arrived, I was back at First Baptist along with the three preachers from my days at Carroll Street. Two families from my time at Southgate Baptist had also joined the church of my youth. I attended a singles' class on Sunday mornings, and I sang in the choir. Often, I would join my parents for lunch after the morning service.

The love and support from our church connections was amazing in helping us to deal with such a painful experience. Our Minister of Music graciously allowed me to sing a solo during the last service my mother attended. On Mother's Day weekend, in 1985, the Lord called her home.

I had lost my best friend — the one person in my world who I knew loved me more than life itself. I was not sure how I could go on without her. I also knew that it was time for me to step up and be the strong one. My dad was breaking apart into small fragments of the man I once knew. His world had crumbled, and he had become more fragile than I knew was possible. My time to grieve would have to wait. I had to put my father back together again, one piece at a time.

After my mother's death, I became more active in church, from teaching a Sunday School class to playing the piano for Sunday morning assemblies. I even joined the bell choir. I agreed to chair the flower committee, which was responsible for the weekly worship service floral arrangements. I loved the chance to be creative and was known for a few over-the-top productions.

That spring, I cut down two slender dead trees from the woods behind our home. I loaded one in the back of my car and took it to the church. I ran back home and loaded up the second and left a trail of debris as I carried then into the sanctuary. Using stands designed to hold flagpoles, I placed the trees on each side of the pulpit, one behind the piano, the other behind the organ. For that Sunday, the trees stood bare for the service. The church was abuzz with curiosity.

Before the next week's service, I used a hot glue gun to attach pink silk dogwood blossoms onto the bare branches, creating a light and airy look. Again, there was much discussion about the two 12-foot trees that now appeared to be in bloom.

It was the following week when it all came together. I taped trays filled with OASIS foam blocks and moss along the half-wall that ran in front of the choir loft, and gathered dozens of assorted cut flowers to fill the trays. It turned into a stunning spring garden, running the length of the stage area, still anchored by the two pink dogwood trees. Oh, how I would have loved for my mother to have seen my creation.

The flower committee was a three-year commitment that left me a bit overwhelmed when added to my other church obligations. Never wanting to let anyone down, I just kept saying yes when asked to help. My breaking point, for no apparent reason, finally came when I was asked to host a Sunday School class party in my home. No one else had stepped up — why would they when they knew I would do it? Feeling pulled in every direction, I decided this would be my last commitment. I had to make it stop, and yet, I did not know how to say no. I could have, or should have handled it better, but the only thing I could think to do was to walk away. And so I did.

I would still occasionally join my dad in the balcony for a worship service — but more often than not, I'd simply meet him for lunch after he attended the church service. When he passed away in the year 2000, I held his funeral in the church that he loved. Although I do have wonderful memories from my years at First Baptist, they are clouded by the fact that this is the place where my childhood innocence was stolen, by three different men, over and over again. As hard as I have tried, I find that I am unable to forgive, and thus, unable to forget.

I have never given up on the Lord, and I know he has not given up on me — but in regards to the Southern Baptist church — **I. Am. Done.**

EIGHT

MY WORLD IN THE TIME OF AIDS

Before I ever opened my first art gallery, a close friend introduced me to Ken Kinsley's artwork. I can remember her unrolling canvases on the floor of my Christmas shop for me to see. Ken mainly worked in oil and was known for his vibrant colors and heavy texture. His *Diner Series* had received an excellent review from our local art critic, Clara Hieronymus. I fell in love with his work, and once we finally met, felt the same about him. I treasured his friendship.

I would hang the occasional art show in my former second-floor apartment above our Mistletoe Shop. I called the space The Upstairs Gallery, and Ken was one of the few artists I offered a solo exhibition. For that show, he had a wonderful collection of unframed figure drawings on paper, several of which had angel wings. In fact, Ken was one of the first local artists to paint angels, long before the craze began. He had begun working part-time in our shop and may have been influenced by the multiple rooms of Christmas inventory.

I continued to represent Ken when I opened my gallery across the street. This enabled me to place his work in the homes of many of my design clients. Being very adept at figures, Ken suggested I promote his portrait commissions as well.

One of the first commissions I sold was to my dear friend, Debbie Pitts. We had met through church, where she and her husband attended the Sunday School class my parents taught for young married couples. Debbie was artistic, creative, inventive and always eager to learn. And she believed in me. One day, when we were having lunch, I shared with her my desire to open an art gallery showcasing local artists. Without hesitation, she pulled out her checkbook and asked how much it would take to make that happen. She then proceeded to write a check for twice that amount! Construction began, and before long the gallery was open. I represented 30 local artists, including my dear benefactor's pottery, artwork and hand-painted tuxedo jackets.

Debbie then hired me to design an addition to their home as well as redecorate the interior. When she mentioned wanting a portrait, I brought Ken to her home, where he took out his pencil and pad and drew sketches that would be the basis for the portrait. Debbie and her young daughter sat on the sofa reading a book together. Like me, Debbie fell in love with Ken's gentle personality and amazing talent. She was very pleased by the finished portrait, which became the focal point of her newly redecorated room. We lost Debbie several years ago to an unforgiving disease, and to this day, I still miss her sweet smile and the way she could light up a room.

Ken suggested painting a portrait of me that could be used as a sample of his work. I told him that by the time he made me look thinner, younger and darkened my hair, (like I saw myself in my imagination) no one would think he had skill because it would not look like the real me. Ken had not met my mother, but he had seen my photos capturing her beauty. He asked me if it would be okay if he painted her instead. I loved the idea and proceeded to gather my photos, once again, for another portrait.

I had given an anniversary party for my parents the year before my mother was struck with cancer and had picked out the striking red dress that she wore. I asked Ken to paint her wearing that dress, with "the" diamond necklace. From the assorted photos as well as through my eyes, he was able to capture my mother's beauty, inside and out.

After my mother passed away, we donated her clothing, with the exception of the red dress captured so beautifully in that portrait. My father took comfort in having her red dress, hanging in her empty closet, until his death.

My dad's birthday fell on November 3 and my mother's on November 4. As long as I could remember, they had celebrated together. I knew this birthday, without her, would be difficult for him, so I decided to throw a party that November 1985 for his 64th birthday. I invited several of my parents' closest friends. Ken was able to finish the portrait just in time for me to have it on view the night of the party. Women openly wept when they saw the painting and remarked how it looked as if my mother could speak. It was a bittersweet moment for my dad, but a blessing as well.

As for my mother's diamond necklace: In the middle of Christmas Eve dinner, at the home of dear friends, someone rang their doorbell. My dad said it was for him and quickly went to open the door. We all knew better than to question his actions. The following morning, as he and I sat by our Christmas tree, opening presents, I opened a box that took my breath away. He had taken my mother's diamond necklace — made into a ring for me — that the jeweler delivered on Christmas Eve. As stunning as the ring was, it was the fact that it had been her necklace, along with his thoughtful surprise, that meant the world to me. Months later, on a hot summer day while I was at work, someone broke into my West End condominium. I had not worn my ring that day, and because of the robbery, I would never have the chance again.

After my mother passed away, I wrote this song in her honor. I regret never being able to sing it for her.

YOU WERE THERE
for my mother

You were there, from beginning to end, always my friend,
strong as the wind, with faith that would not bend.

You were there, when I was in a bind, with open heart and mind,
support I'd always find, in words that were so kind.

You were there, even when I went away, to help me through each day,
I'd think of what you'd say, you know, you made me this way.

And you loved me, whether I was wrong or right,
Good or bad, day or night.
And now, what am I supposed to do?
Life without you, I'll never make it through,
Oh God, how I miss you.

And now, it's time for me to go, somehow, I think you know,
Your love in me will grow, and through me, your life will show.

You were there.

My dear, talented friend Ken Kinsley lost his battle with AIDS in 1991. Although he was in a relationship, it was old friends of his who took him in and cared for him. They would call me with updates and horror stories about his treatments, and the added pain his partner was putting him through. We all felt so helpless. After Ken lost his battle, I was told his partner swooped in, playing the role of the grieving widow. Maybe he had regretted his actions and maybe, just maybe, he did mourn Ken's passing. It was a frightening time. I now realize that it was not fair to judge anyone on how they chose to react during those dark times.

Turn them loose, set them free.
Stop loving, a memory.

Shortly after my mother passed away in 1985, I went to New York and did something foolish and risky. I saw in a local publication listings for escorts in the area, and there were several names I recognized because of their celebrity. One in particular was Casey Donovan. He was a well-known actor for the 1971 gay cult film *Boys in the Sand*. It was one of the first adult films to go mainstream, not unlike *Deep Throat*, which had played at the Midtown Cinema on Church Street, practically next door to the Paramount Theater of my youth.

I had subscribed to *After Dark* magazine, which ran stories about theater, cinema, stage plays and ballet. There would also be articles about various artists, singers, actors and actresses. I had become familiar with Casey Donovan through that publication. And I knew that his real name was Calvin Culver. I was also slightly familiar with escorts, as I had mistakenly picked one up when I was 16, causing me to run when I realized he expected payment for services rendered.

I called the number in the ad and could hardly believe I was speaking with Casey. We made an appointment for the following night at my hotel. I was a nervous wreck, not knowing what to expect. It was all I could think about the following day. That evening, at the time he was supposed to arrive, the phone in my hotel room rang. It was the concierge in the lobby asking if I was expecting a guest. I did not realize, but after a certain hour, you could not ride the elevator without a room key. The gentleman requested I come down to the lobby to escort my guest.

Calvin Culver
Apt. 5B
406 W. 51st
NYC 10019
(212) 581-2902

That was the longest and shortest elevator ride. I was anxious to see him, and at the same time having second thoughts. I don't know what I expected, but it wasn't what I found waiting for me. He looked like an Ivy League model, at a time when the Preppy look was very much in style. With his blonde hair, khaki pants, brown leather belt and penny loafers, a blue oxford cloth button down shirt and horn-rimmed glasses, he was perfection.

I became like a bashful schoolgirl in his presence. We made small talk on the elevator ride back to my floor, and once we were in the room I offered him a drink. I admitted this was my first time to hire someone and was not sure what was expected or where to begin. He was gracious, funny and absolutely charming. I sat on the bed, and he sat in the chair as we talked. I told him that I had first become aware of him through *After Dark*. And to appear in the know, I told him that I knew his name was Calvin Culver. He asked about me, and I shared that I owned a Christmas shop in Nashville. He acted as if that was the most wonderful thing and told me that he collected ornaments. I said that I would love to send him a "Nashville" ornament when I got back home. With that, he turned over a card advertising the hotel's hair salon and wrote down his address.

He then sat down beside me on the bed and began to kiss my neck. He was gentle and caring and I felt, truly felt, he wanted to be there with me. Yes, I know he was an actor and yes, I know he was being paid. But he played his role convincingly. In fact, at one point, as I was staring into his face, I said: "I can't believe I'm here with Casey Donovan." To which he replied: "And I can't believe I'm here with Ron York from Nashville."

I did send him a couple of ornaments when I got home and in return, he sent me a lovely thank-you note. If all encounters with professional escorts were as perfect as my night with Casey, then I could understand why some people choose to hire someone over the trials and tribulations that can come from dating. It's easy to judge, but I would imagine there would be some who if given the chance to spend an evening with someone that they always thought of as just a fantasy, they would be opening their checkbooks, too.

Casey Donovan died two years after my mother, in 1987, at the age of 43 from HIV. I made my first appointment at the local Health Clinic. A close friend went with me as I had myself tested. It seemed like an eternity waiting to learn the results. I was so grateful when I received the news that I tested negative.

On a trip to New York the following year, I looked across a piano bar and saw a stunning man staring at me. I nodded, and he came over and bought me a drink. His name was Marty, and as we talked I felt ever so out of my league. Educated and handsome, he was an opera buff and had even become friends with the legendary Beverly Sills. He also loved design, was accomplished at faux finishes, and was an authority on anything relating to Beaux Arts architecture.

I invited him back to my hotel and was in disbelief when he stayed the night. We continued to keep in touch, and once he came to Nashville to visit me. I threw a huge party while he was in town, although I felt I needed to have a big stick to keep my friends at bay. I took him to the Hermitage, the home of President Andrew Jackson, but he was clearly disappointed. The house seemed so plain to him and it is, if you compare it to the gold-leaf-gilt luster of French architecture. Still, it was a magical weekend.

We kept in touch, but long distance relationships seem doomed from the start. I did connect Marty with the sister of my dear friend, Debbie, who had subsidized my art gallery. Her sister lived in New York, and through my connection she contracted Marty to work his magic on her home. I got to visit Marty a couple of times when I returned to New York. His former partner had contracted AIDS, and he was concerned and went to be tested. When he tested positive, he immediately let me know. Once again, I set up an appointment at the health clinic and, once again, I tested negative. But I did not feel like rejoicing when my beautiful friend was struggling.

I got to visit Marty one last time and found him weak and pretty much confined to his apartment. He was still handsome, although much thinner. We kept the conversation light, and he showed me a photo of Beverly Sills from when she had come to visit him. Shortly after my visit, I learned he had passed away.

This was a period of time during which I lost several friends and friends of friends to AIDS. A beautiful young man from church had returned home, with his body ravaged by the effect of AIDS. I had heard his father was having a hard time with: one) his child was dying; and two) the stigma the disease carried. I told my dad I wanted to visit him in the hospital. His first response was negative, then fear, then acceptance. He accompanied me to the hospital, and I put on the protective gear and sat with my friend. My dad remained in the hall with my friend's father. I think my dad's presence did more good than mine. I don't know what they talked about, but the fact my friend's father saw another father and fellow church member with a gay son and that he was clearly willing to support them, most likely made him realize he was not alone.

I lost several other friends to that dreaded disease. One of which, I learned, continued to meet young men, have sex with them and not admit that he was positive. Our friendship ended when I told his latest conquest to be sure to practice safe sex. I don't know how many men he might have infected, but I knew I could not stand by and not say anything.

HIV POSITIVE

It was several years ago, when I first, heard that word.
I think I saw it on the news, or maybe it was something I read.
I really don't remember, except I know, it made me cry.
The story touched my heart, but soon it was forgotten.

And then I heard, a friend of a friend, knew someone who was dying.
It seemed to be coming closer, almost a reality.
But still, I knew, it couldn't be me, No, it wouldn't be you.
Still, the story touched my heart, but soon it was forgotten.

Now I know, so many friends, struggling to win the fight.
You know, I've even lost a few, it's still so hard to believe.
And when I hear those who ridicule, it really makes me mad.
For their stories touch my heart, and never will be forgotten.

Why can't we understand? Why can't we lend a hand?
Why can't we share the pain? Why must we point the blame?
Why must someone accuse? Why must someone abuse?

It could have easily been me. Why did it have to be you?
I'd rather lose you to another lover, than to lose you this way,
You know I won't recover.
Still our story has to be known, even if I have to tell it, on my own.

Let us, try to understand. Let us, lend a hand.
Let us, try to share the pain. No longer, point the blame.
Let this story touch your heart, and never be forgotten.

♫

I began to focus more on my design career and eventually let the Mistletoe Shop go. It had never been the same since my mother's illness and death. I rented a space across the street and opened an art gallery in 1990. It began as a co-op, where I would rent a wall to an artist and take a smaller commission on sales than the other galleries. Within the first year I had expanded, doubling the size of the gallery, to the point at which I represented over 130 local artists.

I was active with my interior design career and worked with clients and their homes throughout Nashville, Washington, D.C., Texas and Florida. I drew plans for home additions as well as complete residences. My largest project built from my design was an 11,000-plus square foot Georgian residence in the Oak Hill area of Nashville.

I had several employees in the gallery and frame shop, but I alone handled the design clients. The businesses worked hand in hand, and I could not have been more pleased. Even my father was supportive and helpful. He would usually play devil's advocate with each change but would eventually get on board. Our relationship grew stronger, and I'd hear from his friends how proud he was of my accomplishments.

My dad had two very rough years after my mother passed away. He had found the love of his life and did not know how to cope without her. He began drinking more and eating less, so that any drinking would lead to drunkenness. Several of his friends expressed concern.

My dad was so lonely that one night he invited himself to join "Jay," "Dan" and me for dinner. I was pleased he was accepting of my friends. I'm not sure if he ever put it together that it was "Jay" on that fateful Sunday afternoon who had called him in retaliation after my mother and I had been to his home to pick up my furniture. Even though he felt comfortable around my friends, he would still become very protective if he thought someone was trying to take advantage of me.

I wrote my dad a song, and I was able to sing it for him, unlike the song I wrote for my mother. With tears in his eyes, he said that I had captured what he felt.

Ron and Bob York

I THANK THE LORD FOR THE MEMORIES
for my father

Well, the old friends check on me, and I say I'm doing fine.
They say, it's gonna be alright, it's just gonna take some time.
Well, I guess I'm glad they worry, now that I'm all alone,
but with all their good intentions, silence echoes through our home.

After all the years together, I'm left with a broken heart,
We said for richer or poorer, in sickness and health,
Till death, till death due us part.

Well, the old friends say there's someone, I want you to know.
You've got so much in common, give it a try, well, who knows?
But there could never be another, in this world to take your place,
So, I silently wait, until the time, once again, I'll see your face.

Well, I thank the Lord for the memories, of the years, both good and bad,
A lifetime spent, just loving you, well old friends envied what we had.
And I'll take those years of memories, we shared as husband and wife,
And lock them away, down deep in my heart,
As they carry me through, the rest of my life.

♫

Through the years, I had an unusual collection of employees. In the beginning days of owning a gallery, I shared space with a framer who juggled one possible boyfriend with one impossible, and married, boyfriend. The result often left me making excuses for her and learning of her sexcapades that happened in the gallery after hours. Eventually, she moved on, and another framer took her place. This one was an attractive married man with several children. He had the knack of disappearing at a certain time most days. I pressed him for an excuse and learned he was stepping out to attend a *Sexaholics Anonymous* meeting — and then he added that he was attracted to me. I thought, how should I respond? Seriously, what are the rules of etiquette in this situation?

I hired a few artists to help and learned one would meet my customers, then work out a plan to sell to them directly, cutting the gallery out of its commission. And then came "Ben." I had first met him at a friend's party when he was in a relationship, but that did not stop me from finding him attractive. We reconnected after that relationship ended, as he was in need of a part-time job. I hired him, and he made for an excellent employee. One day, I crossed the line and made a pass at him — he responded favorably, and for the next several months we would get together in the gallery or at his apartment.

I can look back now and recognize my pattern. I knew he liked a certain artist, so I gave him a large painting for his home. I asked him to attend an event with me, but he did not have a suit. And yes, I took him shopping. We did not have a conventional relationship, but I thought we were having fun.

I was totally blindsided by a comment a mutual friend made to me, however. He said "Ben" was uncomfortable at work and that he did not want a relationship. He felt I was forcing myself on him. Had I been that blind to not pick up the signals? I still don't remember any resistance from him. Did he really say he was fearful of his job and therefore went along with whatever I wanted? Having been in that position myself, I would never want to make anyone else as uncomfortable as I had been. Or was my friend just jealous and telling me lies?

I asked "Ben" if what I heard was true. He did not deny it but also did not give me any encouragement that he wanted to continue. I was floored. How could I have not noticed any signs that my affection was not wanted? I apologized to him. But also, I had a hard time accepting that I had done anything wrong.

Then again, I had been in his position, when I was employed at a church and had played along to keep my job.

I WANT MORE

The first time I saw you, you were with, someone else.
And I thought, to myself, what a lucky man, he must be.
You stayed together, for such a long time, and I, I never let my feelings show.
But in my dreams, my fantasy, I was wishing, you were with me.

Now that you're on your own, I wanted to make my move.
Although, it was quite by accident, your response, has changed my life.
Play it cool, I said to myself, but I, I couldn't hide the truth.
So here I am, I'm begging for more, and wishing, you were with me.
Now that I've had, a taste of your love, the fantasy becomes real.
I thought that I could handle, a one night stand, but I was wrong.

'Cause I want more, I want more of your love,
I want more, I want more of your time,
I want more, I want more of your love,
Please give me more, give me more, of you.

The first time I saw you, you were with, someone else.
And I thought, to myself, what a lucky man, he must be.

NINE

PHOTOGRAPHER — PORNORGRAPHER

An interesting encounter with a customer at my gallery in the early 1990s led me to take up photography. He was there for framing and I thought he was very striking, with dark long hair and beard. He resembled the pictures of Jesus from my youth. In conversation, he mentioned that he modeled for drawing classes and indicated that he would be happy to do so for me. Although I was having success with my painting, I told him I did not think I had the skills to draw him. My colorful, whimsical acrylic paintings were selling well, but as a self-taught artist, I knew my limitations. He then said there had been times when he posed for photographers. I laughed and said all I had was a Polaroid — this was long before digital cameras. You can imagine my surprise when that did not deter him, and he asked when I wanted to get together.

The next night, after hours at the gallery, this modern-day Jesus disrobed and posed for me as I tried to concentrate and keep my hands from shaking as I snapped Polaroids of him. It was clear he was an exhibitionist and enjoyed having his body worshipped. I was more than happy to oblige.

The experience did give me the incentive to enroll in a photography class at Watkins College of Art, located on the upper floors above the W.T. Grant store, where I spent untold hours in the men's room during my preteen summers.

I purchased a decent camera and enjoyed the beginner class. Figure study was taught in the more advanced course, but after expressing an interest to my teacher, he suggested I go ahead and give it a try. He told me to bring my photos in for him to critique. I did not have to be told twice.

Meanwhile a fellow artist who worked at my gallery in 1992 began discussing my photography class. I told him that I was not yet comfortable asking anyone to pose, since I felt I was an amateur. He said he'd be happy to pose for me and thought his girlfriend might as well. They became my first models, unless you count my earlier "religious" experience one night with a modern-day Jesus and a Polaroid camera.

I called this artist "Convertible," because he had dropped by one day to apply for a job and could not have been any more adorable or personable. When he walked out, an employee who had witnessed everything watched from the front window as he headed to his car, a convertible, and she said: "If he gets in and puts that top down, I might have to leave my husband and run off with him." I called "Convertible" the next day and offered him the job. I was quite pleased with the results from the photo session and also comfortable working with "Convertible" and his girlfriend. I kept everything very professional, although my first instinct, when "Convertible" took off his clothes, was anything but professional.

I began to feel more confident with my abilities. I let it be known that I was looking for models and was amazed by the response. The son of one of my design clients had begun to work for me at the gallery. He was handsome

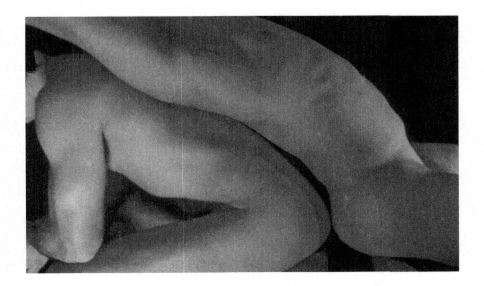

and had a very athletic body. He was more than happy to undress for the camera and became my most frequent model. He encouraged his younger brother to pose for me and came to the appointment to support him. The brother stayed in his boxer shorts for some time, and I thanked him for posing but said I had done all I could as long as he stayed dressed. His brother, making it competitive, finally convinced him to strip. I was able to achieve stunning photos of the two of them together. So much so that their mother, my design client, purchased a pair of framed photos for each of them. She went so far as to help finance a book of my photography released in 1993 called *Nudes and Nonsense*. Although the book is now out of print, the photographs live on.

This employee accompanied his mother and me when I worked on designing their Florida condo. He and I shared a bedroom, which allowed me to easily wake him at daybreak one morning. We drove down to the deserted beach, where he took off his clothes and I captured the early morning sun glistening off his body. On another trip, we drove around finding empty homes, where he would jump in their pool or lounge on their lanai as I clicked photos, one after another. We had a couple of close calls of being caught, but I think he enjoyed the risk.

That first Florida trip was exciting, because I took the opportunity to work with a model outdoors. Plus, I enjoyed the interior design work as well. My client was well aware that her son and I were planning on doing a photo shoot, but still it seemed to cause a bit of friction. The most uncomfortable thing that happened, and has stuck with me through the years, was something she said one morning. I was showering in the bath off the bedroom her son and I shared. He showered in the master bath and, according to his mother, was taking too long. She then went on to say that she finally had to get in the shower with him to move him along. As my skin began to crawl, I prayed that she was kidding.

Her son and I had an interesting relationship. He was definitely heterosexual but also seemed to enjoy the attention that I offered. It was almost as if he liked letting people think that something sexual going on between us. I can remember asking him to be my date for an art fundraiser where more than half of the attendees were gay. He stayed close to me, attentive and often with his arm around me. He made sure I had a drink or plate of food. There were plenty of partygoers there, with hungry eyes, watching his every move and envious that I was the one clearly receiving his attention that night. It was a definite high for me to be seen with this handsome young man by my side. It was also very enjoyable when our photo sessions escalated into something a little more "hands-on."

I worked with many more models — some were referrals, while others asked to model after seeing examples of my photography. Several of the models were gay, but most were straight with girlfriends or wives. One was even a married choir member from First Baptist Church. Of course, I was well aware of the acts of my fellow church members from my past, as well as from a brief encounter I had with another married church choir member.

Several of the models worked as massage therapists — and I found myself having massages three to four times weekly. Men that worked with the body, such as masseurs or personal trainers, seemed quite comfortable with nudity. One very handsome therapist turned out to be an escort and was more than happy to undress for the camera. I did not realize that he also acted, but some months later I had to smile when seeing him appear as Jesus in a Christmas music video for a local Christian singer. With the models' permission and signed consent forms, I submitted photos to *Playgirl* magazine for their amateur model section and was published internationally four times.

I was unknowingly moving from art into something much more risky. I realize now that I did not hesitate for a minute when one model asked me to film him in a solo sexual situation. I had a video recorder and a willing model. He had wanted it for his personal use, but I told him I thought there was a market for this type of thing. Intrigued, he wondered what the financial gain might be. I researched and found an out-of-state company that marketed amateur videos, including the antics found on the New Orleans' streets during Mardi Gras. I wrote to them and asked if they would have interest and included a photo of the model. It turned out that they were very interested, anxious and willing to pay.

My employee and model was not interested in doing a video himself but liked the idea of the extra income that might result from sales. He offered to put the business in his name, which helped eliminate any reservations I had. I was not the least bit computer savvy at the time, so he helped with the correspondence. We needed a name for the business and the first name chosen was after my car brand. Eventually, we changed the name to my brand of shaving cream!

It all started with an innocent photography class — photos of nature and architecture, then to my interest in figure studies. Tasteful nudes moved into something more suggestive and erotic as the opportunity of being published in *Playgirl* came about. Explicit photo sessions led to romantic, and yes, sexual encounters with my models. And then, solo videos that started off artistic reached the point to which I simply accepted and created the straightforward porn that was in demand. This was an adult version of my childhood progression of being sexually abused at age 7 in church, then at age 10 in the downtown movie theaters, followed by the department store restrooms at age 12, and on and on until my breakdown in high school.

I let myself not only go up to the line but cross over as if it did not exist. The model who had led me down this road envisioned a possible career in pornography, and I was helping him achieve that. I was an adult whose childhood had been one full of secrets and without boundaries. This did not seem like a big leap from where I had been in the past. There was only a slight warning light flashing in my brain with concern for my gallery business, if this became known.

♫

I was able to acquire a list of models from the faculty at Watkins College of Art. The models posed for the figure drawing classes. But what can make an interesting subject for a drawing might not work as well on film, which is less forgiving. There were a few models physically in shape that allowed me to expand my repertoire, however. In fact, I worked with a total of 53 models, including seven female models.

Since I hired the models sight unseen, it was always a surprise when I opened my door. There was one model from that list took my breath away. He was a Vanderbilt divinity student and had the face of an angel. Our first session only netted portrait photos, as I could not stop pointing my camera at his face. Eventually I made myself photograph the rest of his body and drink in his entire beauty. He was another of my recurring models, and he knew I found him very attractive. After one of our many sessions, this heterosexual student was willing to engage in sex, saying he felt it was something he should experience.

Then there was "Tom," who had placed an ad in the *Nashville Scene* paper for massage services. His studio was near my gallery, and I made an appointment with him. I was smitten from the first meeting. "Tom" was an outgoing jock who had modeled and acted in a few music videos. I learned he was also a personal trainer, and I hired him on the spot. I talked with him about modeling for me and set up an appointment. He was another male that was comfortable undressed — and if I looked like him, I would be, too. I continued to receive weekly massages and worked out at the gym with him twice a week. Plus, I hired him to model, so it felt as if I had him on payroll. Never once did I mind writing those checks, or paying double at one point, when I was fortunate enough to have "Tom" and the divinity student model together. It was an amazing experience photographing these two stunning models — watching them interact with each other in such a comfortable, suggestive way.

"Tom" eventually moved in with me. I knew it would be temporary, because he had his heart set on the bright lights of Broadway and planned to move to New York. I loved having him share my home even though he slept in the spare room. He had the ability to make me, and anyone around him, feel good. He would start conversations with strangers and they ended up as old friends. We were able to get away to Sanibel Island, Florida, a couple of times, and my college friend Billye joined us on one getaway. I did not want to admit it, but my heart and mind had fallen for this young man, 16 years my junior.

One morning, when "Tom" was leaving for work, he quickly kissed me on the mouth, something he had not done before, and said goodbye. I was so stunned that all I could say in return was: "Have a good day." But from that point on, kissing became a very natural part of our relationship. As you would expect, I fantasized about our life together. My composition from

college 25 years earlier still rang true. I could barely enjoy living in the moment for *"Dreamin' of things to come."*

JUST WHEN I THOUGHT

Just when I thought my life was in order, and everything was in it's place.
I had adjusted, to my life alone, content to slow down the pace.

Just when I thought, my heart had turned cold, and I had lost all desire,
You softly spoke, some magical word, and ice turned into fire.

When you came through my door, not knowing what was in store.
My heart skipped a beat and my knees became weak,
My throat was so dry that I could not speak,
That's when I knew my life was going to change.

Yes, I knew, oh I knew, the minute I saw your face.
It was you, it was you, and it's time to pick up and get back into the race.

I mentioned the idea of solo videos to "Tom," the divinity student and to other models. Many were intrigued by the idea. Since "Tom" lived with me, I had more time with him and thus created more solo videos of him. The company that marketed the videos could not get enough of "Tom," so I was continuously trying to think of new angles to make it interesting. We had sessions in our home, my gallery, and unbeknownst to my dad, in his office after hours. My favorite videos happened on one of our Florida trips — sunshine, beach, pool and even parasailing showcased his muscular frame. We added a few minutes of him driving nude along the bridge leading to Sanibel Island, in a sexy convertible. I loved being able to mix work with pleasure.

Sadly, my time with "Tom" came to an end in 1995 when he made the decision to finally pack up and move to New York. I was devastated when he pulled his car out of my carport and drove away. Between what was real and the fantasy playing in my head, I was beside myself. He was for the most part heterosexual, but with me he was something else. We lived together and often ate together, we worked out together, swam together, traveled together. We exchanged massages regularly. He modeled for me, performed for me, kissed me, hugged me and occasionally shared a bed with me. It was not a conventional relationship, but it worked for me and was less dysfunctional than my previous relationships. There was less drama surrounding him. Being with him felt normal and easy. He was affectionate, protective, and never gave me the feeling he expected anything more from me emotionally or financially. He was fun to be around, and by being so outgoing, he would make me want to be as well.

For our last weekend together, we drove to Chattanooga and stayed in a train car at the historic Chattanooga Choo Choo Hotel. We toured the Tennessee Aquarium, shopped, ate, and enjoyed each other's company. I started to break down emotionally on the trip home, knowing he would be leaving the next day. But he comforted me, and that gave me the strength to drive on.

He went to visit his family in Oklahoma before heading to New York that summer of 1995. He stayed with his younger brother for a few weeks, and during that time I sent him a letter but did not receive a response. Finally, I called his brother's home and asked to speak with "Tom." When his brother realized who I was, he became very rude. I longed to talk with "Tom" and had no idea why his brother was so hostile to me when he did not even know me.

About a week later, I received a letter from "Tom" that explained what was going on. His brother had opened the letter I had sent to him and after reading it, he did not understand why I would be saying intimate things to his big brother. "Tom" wrote that he had come clean to his brother about what had been going on. His brother did not understand and was conflicted between the love he felt for his big brother and the idea that "Tom" had been in a relationship with a man. In the letter, he told me it was not my fault and not to think I had done anything wrong. His brother was the one having the problem — plus, he should have never opened his mail in the first place.

"Tom" finally made it to New York and worked as a personal trainer while he studied acting. We talked a couple of times, but then I was unable to reach him. I made a trip to New York, and since I had his address I went by his apartment. I slipped in the locked door of the building behind a tenant. I easily found his apartment and knocked on the door. A young man opened the door, and I explained I was a friend from out of town and asked if he was there. The young man told me "Tom" had moved out the previous week and offered to let me leave a note for him. The apartment was small and there were two sets of bunk beds, leading me to believe four people shared the space. I wrote a simple note, saying I was in town and the name of my hotel. I never heard from him. I think now that I may have just been a detour for him and that he is now back on his intended path.

WAKE UP BLUE

I go to sleep, thinking of you.
I have sweet dreams, all the night through.
Then morning comes, tell me what should I do,
Without you here, I always, wake up blue.

Put your arms around me, and hold me tight.
Kiss me and tell me, everything's alright.
And say you love me, as I turn out the light.

Your side of the bed is empty and cold,
I embrace your pillow, just for something to hold.

And I go to sleep, thinking of you,
I have sweet dreams, all the night through.
Then morning comes, tell me what should I do.
Without you here, I always, wake up blue.

Eventually, I ran out of models willing to be filmed. But the company kept wanting more. I could not place an ad in the paper and did not want to ask someone, unless I felt confident they would be interested. A budding porn business was not something my partner and I wished to announce to the public.

It was the mid-1990s, and there were still certain areas downtown where willing young men would nod as you drove by, letting it be known that their time and body could be purchased. I had always been aware of that, even more so once I started taking the photography course. Several of my assignments had to do with architecture, light and angles. I would ride around downtown on Sundays, when the streets and businesses were deserted, and take photos of the light reflecting off of buildings. Often there would be some of the "working" men and women out on certain corners eagerly watching for the next passing car.

With my video camera in the car, I decided I'd take a chance and see if I could hire a hustler and turn him into an actor. I shiver now at the risks I took when unlocking my car door and letting in a stranger. The first few times were awkward. It took a few moments to make them understand that the video I wanted to shoot was solo. I would only be holding the camera and definitely not participating. The going price for the "talent" was $40 but each segment was fairly brief, so I had to convince eight different men to let me film them just to make the video long enough to be salable.

Some of the young men were cute, in a rough trade sort of way. A couple of the men made me uncomfortable and one demanded more money — I said I did not have more to give, which was true. Two of the men could not have been sweeter. One seemed refined and educated, leading me to wonder, why be out working the streets, never knowing whose car you are getting into, or who might be an undercover cop? Was he that down on his luck, or just enjoying the thrill? But I had educated, employed, religious and even married men willing to pose nude and perform for my camera and be paid for their time. Was picking up a male hustler that much of a stretch from paying a fellow church member to perform for the camera? Clearly, there were those from all walks of life willing to take risks.

Each of the men I picked up knew of an area where they felt comfortable performing for the camera. I can only assume that they had discovered them through trial and error. On Sunday morning through late afternoon many of the locations were deserted. One hustler led me to a spot with industrial warehouses near the Cumberland River. Another led me deep into a wooded area of Fort Negley Park, where he had set up a tent and clearly had been living. A couple preferred to stay inside my car, while another knew of a commercial parking lot near our former baseball stadium. It was educational, but it reminded me of my own discoveries, years earlier, as I sought out the downtown men's rooms.

Several years later, I would see one of the men from my video as he walked past my gallery daily. I assumed he worked nearby. His long hair had become salt and pepper and his face weathered, looking older than I imagined him to be. I'm not aware of any of the men learning who I was or where I worked. I also thought, with that kind of life, they might be transient and move from city to city, especially once our local police began their crackdown on prostitution.

There was one man who asked me to drop him off across the river. He led me deep into one of the low-income housing developments. He told me where to stop and said he needed to pick up something from a friend. He asked me to wait for him. Fortunately my hustler/model was quick, but I realized when he returned that I had given him enough money as well as the transportation to buy drugs. I took him back across the river, dropped him off and felt grateful that nothing terrible had happened. It was in the fall of 1996 that I swore not to put myself in that situation again.

As with my youth — from being molested through the arrest and eventual breakdown — I found myself traveling down the same type of road once again. What began with an innocent photography course had escalated to hiring street whores to make pornographic films. It had to end. I had much more at stake to lose. When I allowed myself to stop and think about it, I knew it was dangerous, risky and wrong on so many levels. So, why did I let it go this far?

I'm circling the block, on the bad side of town.
Looking at the "ladies" as I drive around.
And thinking that I might buy an hour of two,
And they might show affection, the way you used to do.

I'm going, downtown, once again, hoping I might find a new friend.
To get me through this loneliness, just one more day,
And help me, drink your memory away.

T E N

A SUDDEN DEATH

The day before Thanksgiving 1996 I was at the gym ready to cool down on the treadmill after my workout. Something didn't quite feel right, and I told myself I was just tired. I quickly scanned the gym to make sure my trainer had left in hopes that he would not see me stopping after just a few minutes and heading home. I later mentioned to my father about not feeling up to par. He offered to take me to my doctor. I was sure it was nothing serious and said I'd be fine and that I looked forward to Thanksgiving. He had planned a big dinner and invited a few friends to join us the following day.

Thanksgiving morning I felt exhausted. It took all the energy I could muster just to shower and shave. I still managed to arrive early at my dad's home with every intention of helping him with the finishing touches for our Thanksgiving dinner, but my body had different plans. I could not do much more than sit and watch him pull everything together.

Throughout the dinner, he watched me with concern. I left before our guests and fell into bed when I got home. He called to check on me and offered to take me to the hospital, but I felt too weak to bother. The following morning, I could not find the strength to shower and called my dad for help. He rushed me to the emergency room at Baptist Hospital, where they put me in an examination room immediately and began running tests. A doctor came in to explain that I was on my way to a heart attack. I told the nurse my father was in the waiting room, probably coming unglued, and that they needed to bring him back for the explanation.

My dad stood at the foot of my bed and listened to what they were saying. My gruff, strong dad had a look of fear in his eyes that he could not hide. He had lost his wife of nearly 40 years to cancer. Now he was being told he could lose his son.

From there they rushed me into surgery. I was later told I had blockage to half of my heart and had suffered a mild heart attack. I was very fortunate that I had not waited another day, as they assured me it could have easily been fatal.

Four years later, my father had a heart attack while driving that resulted in a single-car accident. He was rushed to the hospital. They kept him alive with machines until I could arrive. By the afternoon, the machines were turned off. I held his hand as he took his last breath.

It was time to say goodbye to the man I loved with all of my heart but who could often make me so mad that I'd dream about moving away to achieve independence. He could be so thoughtful with small gestures. Simple things like dyeing eggs to put in my annual Easter basket — a tradition he continued until he died. I was 48 years old on his last Easter in 2000. That morning, I found an Easter basket in my car with my favorite candy and dyed eggs — along with a small jar of mayonnaise and another of pickle relish so I could turn them into egg salad.

During my college days, my dad would swing by and pick up my dirty laundry that I would leave in my car. I would find everything freshly washed and ironed waiting in my car the following day, often with home-baked goodies or Krispy Kreme doughnuts.

He was also incredibly generous with what he wanted you to have. I may have asked for a certain item or brand but would find he would buy something similar that he liked more or felt might be a better option.

After my mother was diagnosed with cancer in 1984, he wanted to surprise her with a new car. I reminded him how much she had loved that yellow 1962 Cadillac Sedan de Ville. I told him it did not have to be a Cadillac but whatever he chose, it had to be yellow. So he bought her a maroon Mercury Gran Marquis. Yes, it was a beautiful car, but it was the color he loved and not her favorite Miami-sunshine yellow.

I now know that he was a man with a tortured past who faced his demons daily. A man, whose mother passed away when he was 9 years old and whose father married a woman who could never take his mother's place. I learned through my dad's 1936 journal, when he was 14 years old, that his dad had a job that caused him to travel. Many of his daily entries mention, "Daddy still gone."

I seemed at odds with my father for much of my life, but I never felt he did not love me. I did think he did not understand me — but now I know he understood me all too well. The secrets we both held inside might have brought us closer if either of us had chosen to reveal them.

I don't remember ever being so overwhelmed or as exhausted, physically and mentally, as I was by his sudden death. My precious college girlfriend Carol helped me clean my dad's house so my pair of aunts and uncles could stay there when they arrived from Florida for the funeral. So many decisions had to be made, and I felt unprepared. But somehow I managed everything, with the help of several friends.

What did I know, and when did I know it? I had made a discovery, some time back at my parent's home. When my dad traveled, I would often stay at his house. Something had been added a while back that had me curious. A locking doorknob had replaced the original doorknob on the linen closet in my mother's bathroom. Why?

I searched in vain for a key, then figured he must have kept it with him. Since the door opened out into the bath, the hinges were on the outside of the door. I found by taking the pins out of the hinges, you could pull open

The York Relatives

the door from the opposite side of the locked doorknob. I did just that and was surprised to find a few pornographic videos stacked on the shelves. I was even more surprised that there were a few gay videos mixed in with the straight ones. I learned later on that I was not the only one who had made that discovery.

A young man from our church, whose parents were involved in the worship service, would sit with my dad in the balcony on Sunday mornings. He had grown up sitting with him, and my dad thought the world of him and his family. My dad would attend games and other events that this young man participated in and would take him and a friend of his choosing on trips — even to Europe. This young man also had a key to the house.

As I prepared my family home for my relatives' arrival, I checked the linen closet and found it unlocked and the videos gone. Relieved yet startled that he knew about them and that he must have removed them, I asked him if he had a key to the closet, and he said no. But he was as inventive and as curious as me and had taken the hinges off some time ago. That also meant he had seen the porn videos and knew that they were a mixture of gay and straight. I asked him what he thought about that, and he had said my father mentioned one time, in a kidding fashion, not to limit your possibilities.

I also asked him: "Was my father ever inappropriate with you?" He hesitated and said there were a couple of times, when he was about to take a shower, that my dad had said to let him know if he needed him to wash his back. I felt sickened but then realized that the young man still came around and was there helping me. So if there had been something he had been uncomfortable with, it was not bad enough to make him walk away. And yet with the things that happened to me in my youth, I did not walk away, either. Still, I choose to believe it never went that far.

My aunts and uncles arrived for the funeral, and one pair stayed in my dad's bedroom. Some time later, my aunt told me that there had been a pornographic video in his dresser drawer. I don't know if it was gay or straight, because I was not ready to have that discussion with her.

It was not long after the funeral that I began cleaning out to prepare for an estate sale. Then I would put our home on the market. That was when I found the box of letters, the box that led me to investigate a crime and write *Kept in the Dark*, my memoir of family secrets, forgiveness and healing.

♫

At the gallery, I was very fortunate that a friend pointed me in the direction of someone new to town who I hired as gallery director. Scott was overqualified for the job but seemed to enjoy the position. I looked forward to coming to work, and I was confident he would be dependable when I was away. I still had much to do with my dad's estate and business, but with such a wonderful support system I was able to tackle everything and get things settled.

The next few years were uneventful. Or at least, less dramatic than the years that proceeded them. Scott and I handled the gallery, and business was good. I had sold my smaller condominium and the family home and purchased a midsized condo. I had been able to finish it out just as I wanted. I had found a personal trainer who made working out as enjoyable as it would ever be. He was definitely straight, so there was never any sexual tension or a need for me to flirt. The fitness club itself offered other options, however.

We were working out at The Club of Green Hills, at which many years earlier, under different ownership, I had been a member. When I first joined in the 1970s it was called the Cosmopolitan Spa. They opened a location on Nolensville Road near the three-bedroom apartment I shared with John and Larry. It was a beautiful workout center, with indoor pool, sauna, steam room and tanning area. I was young and able to run the laps of the indoor ring that wrapped around the facility. At that time, women and men worked out on alternating days.

One day I ran into a high school classmate at the Spa. I remembered him especially from an incident in the boy's restroom, when he was feeling rebellious in eighth grade. The two of us entered the restroom, and he said: "Watch this." He proceeded to unzip his pants and urinate into the waste can full of paper towels. I stood there watching, at his invitation, and with his permission. It was all I could do to make sure my body did not give away the excitement I felt. Now, 12 years later, I was sitting next to him in the steam room at the health club, both of us in our swimsuits. He was now a construction worker and looked great. Once again, I misread the signals and placed my hand on his thigh. He then placed his hand on mine, and looked into my eyes and said: "Ron, I'm flattered, but I'm not gay. But if I was, I'd be all over you." I was beyond embarrassed and started to apologize. He stopped me and said it's not a big deal, that it's happened to him before. And seriously, he felt flattered that I was attracted to him. He made what was one of my most awkward passes into something very sweet.

A few years later, I began going to the Green Hills location of Cosmopolitan and was surprised by what I found. Being the original location and larger of the clubs, this gym had two dressing areas. It still had the alternating days for men and women for the large dressing room on the far end, over the pool area. But a few steps down on the left side of the front door was a smaller dressing area, where on the off days, you could have access. There were lockers, a tanning area and restroom. There was also a wet area with a whirlpool, larger than the one on the other side. It was placed where you could be in the water, with the jets pulsating around you, and looked directly into the showers, flanked by a sauna to the left and steam room to the right.

I learned that, on the days that the men had the smaller side, it was similar to the gay bathhouses you might find in New York or San Francisco. I also ran into many married men who were there for more than just relaxation. Church members, Baptist Sunday School Board employees, a certain "handsy" music teacher, and more. Sex was rampant on that side. Of course, there also might be the unsuspecting straight men who happened in but left quickly once they realized what was going on. For several years, this was a well-kept secret in Green Hills.

After my father passed away in 2000 and I had joined The Club of Green Hills, I introduced myself to "Rex," the massage therapist, and asked about an appointment and his rates. He told me he did sessions at the club and outcall as well. He pointed out that the noise level of the locker room can sometimes interfere with a client's relaxation, since the massage room opens directly off of the locker room. I opted for a home visit, and we set a time. This handsome young man was only 21 years old and in the military reserves. At 48, I was more than twice his age. He arrived at the appointed time and put up his massage table. I undressed and laid, face down, on the table. I quickly realized he made no attempt to place a drape over me. With only a candle burning for light, he began his massage. I was impressed from the start and slowly began to relax. It was easy to drift away as his hands worked out the stress from my body.

Halfway through, he asked me to turn over. As most men have found with massage, it's not always easy to keep your body from responding to strong hands caressing it with oil. I'll admit to being only slightly embarrassed, and thought if he was uncomfortable, he should have suggested a drape. It became clear he was not uncomfortable at all, and my mind began to wonder as to how this would finish.

"Rex" made sure every muscle was taken care of, which led me to believe he was gay. I asked if I could return the favor. He thanked me but said no, he had a girlfriend and was straight. I did not want to argue, but after that massage, straight was not how I would have described him. I went ahead and made an appointment for another massage.

The second massage went pretty much the same way as the first. But when he arrived for my third appointment he apologized in advance, saying he was tired and not sure how good he would be that evening. I suggested he let me give him a massage. He wasn't sure how to respond, but I assured him I had been trained. When "Tom" lived with me, we would swap massages and I learned from him. In fact, I took on some of his clients for a brief period after he left town. It was fun at first, but then realized I would have enjoyed it more if I could have been more selective with clients.

"Rex" accepted my offer, undressed and stretched out on the table. I lighted the candle, started the music, and began to rub oil on him. When I asked him to turn over, I saw that my work had the same effect on him as his work had on me. By the end of that evening, he barely had enough energy to drive home — and there was no way he could say he was 100 percent straight.

"Rex" and I got together for more than just massage appointments. We would go out to eat or shop at the Bellevue Center mall. He loved to spend the night and always wanted us to sleep naked on the floor in front of the fireplace. My body may have felt too old for that, but my mind and heart were more than happy to hold him through the night in front of a flickering fire.

He was a sweet boy, cuddly like a teddy bear, but he still had a girlfriend and planned on getting married. He even commissioned a painting from me that he gave her as a gift. It was an unusual arrangement, but one that I was accustomed to. I have always seem to attract what I call the "confused heterosexual." In fact, I had much better relationships with men who had wives or girlfriends than with out gay men. But like many straight men who experiment, "Rex" was not comfortable with kissing.

Playing the "other woman" role was something I was comfortable with. Relationships can become complicated, and sometimes the everyday drama gets tedious. My time was often limited and therefore we would make the most of it, whether sexual or simply conversational. For many men, I think I was an escape from their lives. I did not take them for granted and tried to make them feel special by catering to their every whim. In turn, this made most want to return the favor.

Then one night, when "Rex" came over, I could tell something was wrong. He would not admit it, but something had changed. I tried to appease him, but everything I said made him edgy and argumentative. Finally, he blew up, stormed out, and that was that. I tried calling him, but he would not answer or return my calls. Eventually, I stopped trying. I later learned he did indeed marry his girlfriend, and went into the military.

EYES OF A FRIEND

It's the same old story, it's been told, time and time again,
Lonely heart, searching for love, thinks they found it, in the eyes of a friend.

Desperate for attention, longing for just a gentle touch,
Confused heart, dreaming of love, thinks they've found it,
in the eyes of a friend.

The eyes of a friend show compassion,
They show warmth and understanding.
But the eyes of a friend, will never show the love,
Of someone, who's more than just a friend.

Misunderstood, the eyes of a friend, misunderstood, the eyes of a friend.

I continued to work out at The Club of Green Hills with my trainer. There were times I'd lose weight and be in better shape, then times I'd backslide. Whatever my current weight, we would at least have fun.

There was someone that often worked out at the same time as my appointments. Unlike me, he had fallen in love with working out, and the improvements that his body had begun to show. He was an eager student, I appreciated seeing his hard work pay off. My trainer and I would have to laugh when we would see one of the social barflies begin to make their move on him. He always seemed to be clueless that they were coming on to him. I began to view him as a challenge.

The budding fitness model would run the track while I walked at a more leisurely pace. Round and round the circle, he would pass me over and over again. We knew each other's names and would always say hello but never had much of a conversation. One day, after watching his backside pass me time and time again, I complimented him on his calves, which had become more muscular. He seemed surprised and pleased that I had noticed.

My success with the "confused heterosexual" always began with compliments. It is amazing how many men feel the need to be appreciated and complimented. It is easy to take someone for granted and forget the way things were during the courting phase. I'd begin with compliments and then, in time, move on to "safe" flirting. You would be surprised how a man who thinks he is straight in every way enjoys having another man find him attractive. Compliments, flirting — and then, eventually, meet for coffee or lunch.

As I am explaining my approach to seduction, I realize it is similar (if not the same) as a pedophile's approach, in what is known as "grooming" a child. These techniques were used on me and so naturally, I am familiar and comfortable turning the tables. The main difference is a legal one — my conquest is an adult. And now, as I am writing, I am having an *Oh My God* moment in realizing I have been successfully "grooming" straight men for years.

I continued to notice his body's improvements and being vocal about it. Eventually, we started conversing about other things, and I told him about my gallery and photography. I even threw out the idea of him modeling for me. He did not say no. I also learned that he and I shared something unusual in common. We both were given four birth names. I was always unique with my James Ronald Monnie York moniker. And now I had found someone else with four names. I suggested again that Mr. 4-Names model for me. This time he said yes.

We scheduled a time in July 2001 to meet at my home. He seemed comfortable undressing for me, and I kept it professional. He told me later that he knew what I wanted from the start. He was straight, divorced, and was dating, off and on, the daughter of a country music legend. Our first session went well, but the photos were less than stellar. I asked if he